Charles Hamilton

An Historical Relation

of the origin, progress, and final dissolution of the government of the Rohilla Afgans, in the northern provinces of Hindostan

Charles Hamilton

An Historical Relation
of the origin, progress, and final dissolution of the government of the Rohilla Afgans, in the northern provinces of Hindostan

ISBN/EAN: 9783337287269

Printed in Europe, USA, Canada, Australia, Japan

Cover: Foto ©Andreas Hilbeck / pixelio.de

AN HISTORICAL RELATION

OF THE

ORIGIN, PROGRESS, AND FINAL DISSOLUTION OF THE GOVERNMENT OF THE

ROHILLA AFGANS,

IN THE

NORTHERN PROVINCES

OF

HINDOSTAN.

Compiled from a PERSIAN MANUSCRIPT and other ORIGINAL PAPERS,

By CHARLES HAMILTON, Esq.

An Officer in the Service of the Honourable EAST-INDIA COMPANY on the BENGAL ESTABLISHMENT.

SECOND EDITION.

LONDON:

Printed for J. DEBRETT, removed to No. 179, opposite Burlington House, Piccadilly.

M.DCC.LXXXVIII.

PREFACE.

THE following concise history of a People, who, for some time, made no inconsiderable figure in Hindostan, after a delay of many years, is at length presented to the world, at a period when the passions and interests of men being no longer concerned in any of the events of which it treats, it may possibly meet with a more impartial and indulgent reception, than it might otherwise have been supposed entitled to.

But, as some particulars contained in it have been the subject of much acrimonious diſcuſſion, both in England and in India, it may not be improper that the writer ſhould previouſly ſtate the circumſtances which, by poſſeſſing him of the materials, firſt led him at all to think of ſuch a compoſition, as this may ſerve to convince the candid reader, that, in venturing to obtrude this little production upon his attention, he is not actuated by any ſiniſter views, nor by that ſpirit of party, which, unhappily, but too much prevails, even in matters where it ought leaſt to be met with, and where it is moſt prejudicial to the advancement of truth and knowledge; and, in doing this, he will endeavour to ſhun, as much as poſſible, unneceſſary egotiſm, although it muſt unavoidaly compel him to touch upon ſubjects which would otherwiſe be altogether foreign and improper.

Soon

Soon after the author's firſt appointment into the India Company's ſervice (about fifteen years ago) he applied himſelf, with ſome aſſiduity, to the ſtudy of the oriental languages, particularly of that grand medium of all correſpondence and negotiation in India, the *Perſian*; about three years after, he had the honour to be called upon by the officer then commanding that portion of the Bengal army which was on the field ſtation, (who is now in England) for his aſſiſtance in that particular department, for which he had by this time qualified himſelf, to wit, *tranſlation* and *country correſpondence*: Here, as a new field of inveſtigation and inquiry was opened to him, in the probability that he might, in the courſe of his duty, have the management of political buſineſs frequently committed to his charge, he was anxious to acquire ſuch a degree of knowledge of the hiſtory and connections of the neighbouring ſtates, as might enable him to execute matters of that kind in a manner worthy of ſo important a truſt.—It was, at the ſame time, his fortune to meet with a perſon of ſome conſequence, who was an Afgan, then acting on the part of the Rohilla Chief Fyzoola Khan, in a confidential capacity; and from this perſon he procured, (among a number of other valuable papers,) a Perſian manuſcript, containing a compleat relation of the whole Rohilla ſtory, from the firſt foundation of their power, to the battle of Cutterah, fought between the Rohillas and the Allied army of the Company's and Viſier's troops, on the 23d of April, 1774, which, by the defeat of the former, put an end at once to their government and independance.

Pregnant

Pregnant as this appeared to be with many ſingularly ſtriking and intereſting events, the then *recent* tranſactions had, moreover, rendered it an object of particular curioſity, and theſe conſiderations alone were ſufficient to induce the writer to employ his firſt leiſure hours in arranging and turning it into Engliſh: this determination he forthwith proceeded to execute, and, about ten years ago tranſlated the following narrative, in a form and ſubſtance little different from that in which, with becoming diffidence, he now ſubmits it to the public eye.

With reſpect to the motives which induced the writer ſo long to withhold this compilation, before he would hazard to commit it to the judgement of the world, he will not offer to encroach upon the patience of his readers, by mentioning the common-place topics ſo often uſed by many before him, ſuch as, that "the "work was originally written with no "other view than merely the amuſement "of a few friends," and ſo forth; declarations, which are commonly as inſufficient to cover the vanity of an author, as to impoſe upon the penetration of others: —In truth, he always regarded the matter contained in this little tract as by no means unworthy of being made known; but yet, in a point of ſuch moment, he wiſhed not to act with a raſhneſs of which he might afterwards have ſufficient occaſion to repent: nor was he, indeed, leſs deterred by an apprehenſion that, were it to come forth at a period when the conteſt of oppoſite factions, reſpecting the affairs of India, had agitated men's minds to an uncommon degree of animoſity, or whilſt the deciſion of the Legiſlature upon the moſt

moſt intereſting part of its ſubject was yet pending, it might have been regarded as a frivolous FARRAGO, vamped up merely to ſerve the purpoſe of the hour; and, as ſuch, have drawn upon its author ſuſpicions, which, he truſts, cannot, with any ſupport of probability, be imputed to him at preſent.

The particular reaſons which were, for ſo conſiderable a period, obſtructive to his wiſhes and intentions have at length ceaſed to exiſt:—Thoſe events of the following ſtory in which the *Engliſh* were any way concerned have been fully canvaſſed before the higheſt human tribunal; and a judgement from which there lies no appeal ſeems to have been already paſſed upon it.—Neither are the different parties who were principally intereſted in its diſcuſſion now any longer in a ſituation to excite the hopes

hopes of partizans, or the apprehenſions of opponents; ſo that the writer of this little tract preſumes he may ſtand fairly acquitted of any undue bias in the production of it.

But, whilſt ſolemnly diſavowing any intereſt whatſoever in the views either of parties or of individuals in this publication, yet will he venture to confeſs that he is not altogether indifferent in the motives which have led him to it. Concerned for the honour of his country, and anxious for the reputation of a ſervice in which he has ſpent the flower of his life, he would willingly, if poſſible, remove even in a ſingle inſtance, ſome part of that horrid odium which has of late years, for whatever purpoſe, been ſo ſedulouſly excited againſt thoſe devoted men who, at the expence of all the moſt comfortable enjoyments

ments of exiſtence, are rendering the public no unimportant nor unmeritorious (though certainly very *thankleſs*) ſervices in India.

Here, perhaps, the writer might be tempted to enlarge ſomewhat beyond the bounds which the confined nature of his ſubject preſcribes to him, were it not that, in ſuch a diſcuſſion it would be ſcarcely poſſible to avoid animadverſions which, in the eyes of *ſome*, would bear the conſtruction of ſiniſter deſign or of perſonal invective, rather than of the ſober inveſtigation of truth.—Much *abſtracted* reaſoning, indeed, might be advanced on the abſurd *improbability* of the very groſs and univerſal depravity, which has been declared to contaminate the minds of our countrymen in that department of the empire, where they have been depicted,

not

not in the characters of *men*, but of *savages* more fell than the tygers of the region in which they reside. But, in a case of general prepossessions, derived, in many instances, from sources which ought always to *deserve* to be regarded as of the highest authority, it is necessary that time should be allowed for the force of immediate interests to be weakened, and the virulence of contending parties to subside, ere it can be supposed that the admonitions of sober, unimpassioned reason should have any operation in their cure.—He will, therefore, only touch upon this matter at a distance, and merely so far as respects those operations of the English which form a part of the subject of this narrative.

Of all the events which have been made use of for the purposes of crimination against

againſt the ſervants of the Eaſt-India Company, none have made a greater figure, either in the national proceedings, or in the periſhable publications of the day, than the *Rohilla War*, and various efforts have been made to paint both the conduct and the conſequences of it in the moſt horrible colours.

When, in the peruſal of hiſtory, we read of *whole nations* being *extirpated* by the Goths, or *rooted out* by the Vandals, we picture to ourſelves a country invaded by a band of fierce and ſavage conquerors, who purſue the hapleſs inhabitants with indiſcriminate maſſacre, carry off the few they ſpare from the ſword into perpetual captivity, and proceed in their deſtructive career, until the whole territory exhibits nothing but a dreary, ſilent waſte!

Similar

Similar to this is the opinion which, (from the force and extent of the expreſſions that have been applied to it) have been, by many, conceived of the conqueſt of Rohilcund.

God forbid that *Britiſh troops* ſhould ever be employed in acts of ſuch deteſtable atrocity!—With reſpect to thoſe in particular who effected that revolution, it may with confidence be affirmed, that, however high their ſenſe of ſubordination, however ready at all times to obey the moſt perilous orders of their ſuperiors, had ſuch a ſervice been allotted to them, they would have turned from it with abhorrence!

To confute aſperſions ſo cruelly injurious to theſe gallant men is, it muſt be owned, one, and that not the leaſt, of the author's aims; an aim which, when guided by

truth,

truth, he conceives to be neither blameable nor diſhonourable.—He means not, however, to call in the aid of *argument* for this purpoſe: the *facts* follow, and will ſpeak for themſelves: neither is it his buſineſs or his intention to enter into any diſcuſſion of the principles upon which this celebrated expedition was undertaken, as this point muſt be referred to a judgement to be formed upon the ſame grounds: if they were *wrong*, nothing he could here advance would ſuffice to juſtify them; if *right*, it is not in his power to arraign them.

Having premiſed thus much with reſpect to the circumſtances which originally led to this compilation, and the motives for the preſent production of it, it may not be improper to ſubjoin a few obſervations upon the work itſelf.

The

The difficulty of collecting materials capable of forming a regular, connected, and authentic detail of events in the northern parts of Hindoſtan within the laſt century, muſt be well known to all who have ever made ſuch an inquiry the object of their purſuit: the univerſal decline of learning in the empire within that period, has affected *hiſtory* in particular; in the few crude productions of this kind which are to be found, the *dates* of the moſt important events are generally miſplaced, and often entirely omitted; and it frequently happens that no two authors, in the relation of the moſt momentous and intereſting facts, exactly coincide in the points of place and circumſtance: — the writer is therefore ſenſible that his work muſt contain ſome anachroniſms, and perhaps, in a few places, deviations from the relations of others; the *former* of theſe

theſe he has as much as poſſible ſtudied to avoid or rectify; and with reſpect to the *latter*, none that he has been able to diſcover appear of any manner of moment; indeed, he has been the leſs ſolicitous upon this head, as he depends much upon the authority of the perſon under whoſe inſpection (as he has before intimated) the Perſian manuſcript, which forms the chief ground of the work, was drawn up; whoſe knowledge of the ſubject muſt be naturally ſuppoſed to be accurate and extenſive, as he was a *Robilla*, a confidential ſervant of one of their chiefs, and had himſelf been perſonally engaged in many of the events related in it.

The narrative is preceded by a ſhort view of the actual ſtate of the diſtricts of Hindoſtan, ſubject to the Muſſulman governments, as they ſtood at the period of the important revolutions which have been effected by the unparallelled ſucceſs of the Engliſh: this ſketch will, probably, be regarded as very ſlight and imperfect, conſidering the magnitude of the ſubject; the writer, however, is encouraged to offer it, not only as it may tend in general to the illuſtration of what follows, but alſo as it may ſerve to obviate certain miſconceptions which have been, with vaſt labour and ingenuity, raiſed in the minds of the public, and to evince with what peculiar eaſe political revolutions may be brought about in thoſe countries, without inducing any of the dreadful conſequences which have been ſolemnly pronounced (in a place and from an authority too high to be here mentioned) as the conſtant and neceſſary reſult of them.

An appendix is alſo given, containing copies

copies of ſuch original papers as may ſerve the more fully to exhibit thè leading circumſtances of the firſt rupture between our Ally the Vizier Suja-al Dowlah, and the Rohillas, as well as of the treaties of peace which put a period to the calamities thoſe countries, both from their natural and political ſituation, had for many years been ſubject to.

In the original draft of the work, it was termed a *Tranſlation*; both as it was, in fact, in a great meaſure literally ſo, (from the manuſcript, as already mentioned) and alſo, becauſe the writer thought he could thus beſt cover its blemiſhes and imperfections: but, as in ſome parts of it (thoſe, in particular, which treat of ſuch proceedings of the Engliſh government as were any way connected with it) he has neceſſarily had recourſe to other ſources of information, ſo he has thought it moſt ſuitable to drop that appellation, and to ſend it forth under the title of what it really is, a *Hiſtory* or *Hiſtorical Relation*, where all the incidents are combined in their natural connection with and dependance upon each other.

After having ſaid ſo much, it would be unpardonable to treſpaſs farther upon the patience of the reader; yet may the writer be permitted to add that, if in this little publication he ſhould appear to have attempted beyond his ſtrength,—if in addition to the ſeveral defects he is conſcious it contains, the ſuperior penetration of others ſhould chance to diſcover ſtill more, he nevertheleſs hopes that every reaſonable allowance will be made for him; the magnitude and importance of a laborious undertaking, in which he is at preſent engaged

ged, has afforded him but little leiſure for *reviſal* and *correction*, and none for the ſtudy of harmony of language, or elegance of ſtyle, were he even diſpoſed to imagine that his efforts in this reſpect could be attended with ſucceſs ;—to *excel*, therefore, has not been ſo much his aim as to *inform* ; and it is to be preſumed that, in the eye of the candid and the judicious, ſome little credit will be given to the *intention*, even though he ſhould be ſo unfortunate as in any manner to fail in the execution of it.

Some paſſages in the following narrative muſt be intereſting to every Engliſh reader, and, however ſhort its period or confined the ſcene of its tranſactions, yet it may perhaps be found, by ſuch as are deſirous of drawing their concluſions from plain *fact*, rather than from vague *aſſertion*, not to be altogether deſtitute of uſeful and entertaining matter; neither can the hiſtory of a government which underwent the whole progreſſive ſeries of *riſe*, *independance*, and *diſſolution*, within the little ſpace of *Thirty-five* years, be held unworthy the attention of thoſe who, abſtracted from any narrow intereſts or partialities, may be deſirous of deriving amuſement and inſtruction, from a review of the unprofitable toils and tranſitory viciſſitudes of *Human Life*.

A SHORT

A SHORT VIEW OF THE STATE OF THE PROVINCES of HINDOSTAN, SUBJECT TO THE MUSSULMAN GOVERNMENTS; WITH RESPECT TO THE Relative Situation of their INHABITANTS.

IN order to give a more clear and diſtinct conception of this ſubject, it may be neceſſary to premiſe, by taking a curſory retroſpect to the circumſtances, which, through a variety of revolutions effected in the courſe of many centuries, have led to the modern and very ſingular ſtate of thoſe diſtricts which are termed the *Muſſulman Provinces* in India.

In a country of ſuch vaſt extent as *Hindoſtan*, famous from the earlieſt ages for the richneſs of its productions, the ſalubrity of its climate, and the fertility of its ſoil, it is to be ſuppoſed that there are reſidents of all complections, and of every religious perſuaſion: There are, however, only two deſcriptions to be conſidered as forming the grand characteriſtic diſtinctions under which the inhabitants, in general, may be arranged; the *Hindoos* and the *Muſſulmans*, or *Mahommedans*: Of theſe, the former are the *Aborigines*, and the latter the deſcendants of the proſelytes from the Hindoo religion, or of thoſe Arabs, Perſians, and Tartars, who, in the courſe of the laſt eight hundred years, have ſpread themſelves over the face of this extenſive region.

The hiſtories of the Hindoos trace back the annals of an independant ſyſtematic form of government and legiſlation over the greateſt part of this immenſe ſpace to a period far beyond the date of European chronology,

chronology, and pourtray a people flouriſhing in all the ſuperiority of civilized life, at a time when we ſuppoſe the reſt of mankind to have been ſunk (with very few exceptions) into the moſt abject barbariſm. Brave, active, poliſhed, and induſtrious, the Hindoos, in their original ſtate, appear to have been no wiſe defficient in the qualities neceſſary to the defence of their widely-extended territories, againſt the incurſions of the various wild and ſavage nations by whom they were ſurrounded; and, if we are to credit their accounts, and the more unqueſtionable teſtimony of the remains of antiquity which are every were to be found, they enjoyed, for many ages, under a mild and ſimple form of government, founded on a religion whoſe very eſſence ſeems to be benevolence and an abhorrence of blood, a degree of happineſs, the extent and duration of which is not to be equalled in the hiſtory of any other portion of the human race.

Had no events taken place calculated

to

to effect important revolutions as well in the manners of a great part of mankind as in the fate of many empires; had the barbarous hords around this happy region never been actuated by any more forcible impulse than such as the hopes of *plunder* might inspire; it is probable that several centuries might have been added to the felicity and independence of the Hindoos: time, however, and the concurrence of circumstances, have wrought a great change both in the political situation and personal character of this people, in many of the richest and most extensive provinces of their ancient dominion.

The impostor of Mecca had established, as one of the primary principles of his doctrine, the merit of extending it, either by persuasion or the sword, to all parts of the earth. This injunction his followers so steadily adhered to, and so earnestly pursued, that in less than three centuries after its first propagation, a large part of Europe, Asia, and Africa, was seen to embrace

brace or ſubmit to "the law of *the pro-* "*phet*;" and, among the reſt, the northern provinces of Hindoſtan, which had ſo long flouriſhed in tranquil ſecurity, were at length overwhelmed by armies of fierce and hardy adventurers, whoſe only improvements had been in the ſcience of deſtruction, who added the fury of fanaticiſm to the ravages of war, and whom a firm belief in the rewards which, they were taught to expect, awaited all who ſhould be ſo fortunate as to die in the promulgation of *the faith*, inſpired with an energy which nothing could reſiſt. Here, however, the great end of all their conqueſts met with obſtacles ſuch as were no where elſe oppoſed to it; and in India alone, the Muſſulman ſword, although it could overthrow governments and ſubjugate kingdoms, was incapable of gaining or of forcing proſelytes in any proportion to the numbers who were ſubdued: Multitudes were ſacrificed by the ſavage hand of religious perſecution, and whole countries were deluged in blood, in the vain hope that,

that, by the deſtruction of a part, the remainder might be perſuaded or terrified into the profeſſion of Mahommedaniſm: the nature of the Hindoo religion held forth invincible obſtacles to their views: original in its nature, and abſolute in its decrees, its precepts induce a total ſecluſion from the reſt of mankind; and this ſecluſive principle extends not only to the whole of the Hindoos, with reſpect to the reſt of the world, but alſo to every *caſt* or *claſs* of thoſe with reſpect to every other *caſt*:— it neither admits converts from other ſyſtems, nor allows of the ſmalleſt even *temporary* deviation from its own; inſomuch that, if a Hindoo be diſcovered to have ever *eaten* or *drank*, or to have aſſociated in theſe acts with others, contrary to the rules preſcribed to him by his religion (whether voluntarily, or by compulſion) he "*forfeits his* CAST,"— that is to ſay, he becomes utterly baniſhed from ſociety, is conſidered by his friends and relations as dead, and is thenceforth proſcribed as an *alien*, with whom no communication can legally

legally be held : hence every tie which can lay hold upon the heart of man, every enjoyment which conſtitutes his chief delight, are the pledges of a Hindoo's perſeverance in the faith of his anceſtors.—The Muſſulman Princes and Generals who firſt ſucceeded in their attacks upon Hindoſtan ſoon perceived the futility of thoſe ſanguinary efforts, which might extirpate, but could ſeldom *convert*, a people whom neither terror nor intreaty could tempt to deſert a ſyſtem upon their adherence to which their whole happineſs was thus made to depend : they therefore determined to relinquiſh the impracticable ideas with which they had, at firſt, entered upon their career ; and from that period to the preſent time an univerſal toleration ſeems (with few exceptions) to have been the marking characteriſtick of the Muſſulman rules throughout India.

All the countries of Hindoſtan, from the *Indus* to the *Ganges*, were in courſe of time ſubdued by the Muſſulman arms ;

they

they afterwards extended their conqueſts to the eaſtward and ſouthward; all the territories on each ſide of the laſt-mentioned river (as far as the *Cummow* mountains) Bahar Bengal, the Decan and the Carnatick, ſucceſſively fell under the Mahommedans, who ſettled in the countries they had thus acquired, governing them (for the moſt part) in the name and under the authority of the Emperor at Delhi, who was recognized as Lord Paramount over the whole: Many other provinces which never were actually ſubdued, were ſuffered to retain their ancient laws and form of Government, under their own hereditary chiefs, or *Rajahs*, theſe acknowledging fealty to the Muſſulman court at Delhi, and paying tribute to its officers: —Some few, ſecured by their inſignicance, or their inacceſſible ſituation, ſtill continued to retain their former independance.

Thus the Emperors of Hindoſtan held dominion, at one period, over a vaſt Monarchy, conſiſting of diſtricts, provinces, and

and kingdoms, of *two* different defcriptions:— The firft, thofe which, having been conquered by the Muffulmans, were more immediately and completely under fubjection; being protected and held in obedience by Muffulman armies; having Courts of Juftice eftablifhed in them upon the fame principles as in Perfia and other Mahommedan countries, in which all caufes were judged and decided by the ftandard of Muflulman jurifprudence; and governed by Royal deputies or *Nawabs*, whofe occafional appointments took place at Delhi:——The fecond, thofe, which never having been completely fubjugated, ftill retained their ancient laws and ufages, and were governed by *Rajahs*, fucceeding each other, in general, according to lineal defcent; but, liable to ejectment upon any failure, either in the payment of their ftipulated tribute, or the furnifhing of military aid when required, holding their lands, in fact, by a fort of *feudal vaffalage*.

A fyftem fo unwieldy from its extent, and

and compoſed of ſuch heterogeneous parts, could not long be preſerved entire ; and accordingly, the hiſtory of Hindoſtan, for the laſt five hundred years, exhibits little elſe than a continued ſeries of rebellions and inſurrections, and reiterated efforts on the part of the ſupreme government to quell them. The vigorous adminiſtration of a long line of able princes held it, indeed, for ſome time, undiminiſhed; but a few weak reigns undid the work of ages ; and during the decline of the houſe of Timour, within the laſt century, this immenſe fabrick fell rapidly to ruin : Province after province ſeceded from their obedience, and the extent of the imperial authority was gradually circumſcribed, until at length there remained to the deſcendants of that illuſtrious family nothing more than a wretched remnant of territory immediately around the capital, and a ſtill univerſally acknowledged title to royalty expreſſed by inefficient declarations of ſubjection and attachment, which, like the ruins of ſome ſtately pile,

pile, ſerves only to point out the ſplendor it was once poſſeſſed of.

In the diſmemberment of this unwieldy empire, little alteration was made in the interior government or policy of each particular province :—the *Newabs* neglected to remit their revenues to the royal treaſury, and the *Rajahs* witheld their tribute, or renounced their obedience, the countries of each remaining, reſpectively, under the ſame laws, and ſubject to the ſame modes of public adminiſtration as before; excepting only that every chief, as he threw off his allegiance, (in *fact* if not in *terms*,) inſtead of depending any longer upon the appointment of the Court, aſſumed to himſelf the right of eſtabliſhing the ſucceſſion to the dominion of his territory in his own family : each ſucceſſor endeavouring, however, to give oſtenſible validity to his claim, by procuring *Firmans* or commiſſions from the Emperor, to whom all ſtill continued to acknowledge fealty, and to allow the barren privilege of beſtowing nominal honours and marks of diſtinction.

Thus, the empire of Hindoſtan became, and has from that period conſiſted of, a number of kingdoms, provinces, and diſtricts, totally independent of each other, or of any ſupreme head, and of two diſtinct deſcriptions or denominations, *Hindoo* and *Muſſulman*.

Of the former of theſe we forbear to ſpeak, as this view is meant to be confined ſolely to thoſe provinces which, on the general defection, remained, as before, under the dominion of the Muſſulmans; and this, although it particularly points at the territories uſurped by the Rohilla Afgans, may neverthleſs be conſidered as equally applying to all other provinces of the *ſame claſs*.

The Hindoos in theſe diſtricts, although they have loſt much of their priſtine purity and ſimplicity of manners, do yet ſtill

retain

retain the ſtrongeſt marks of an original character.—Their climate, their food, and the delicate conformation of their bodies concur to render them ſoft and effeminate; and the ſingular eaſe with which the earth yields all her productions contributes to cheriſh the natural indolence of their diſpoſitions.—They are brave, but their courage requires an impulſe to ſpur them on to action, which ſeldom offers where all the rewards of military exertion are monopolized by others: they are naturally avaricious; but the total inſecurity of property, whilſt at the mercy of unprincipled and rapacious tyrants, in general, either conſiderably checks this paſſion by diſcouraging its end, or prevents its aſſuming any other ſhape than that of apparent penury, covering the moſt ſecret and moſt ſordid accumulation:—hence, they are little deſirous of improving their ſituation or increaſing their poſſeſſions by any of the bolder or more dangerous purſuits of ambition:—that abaſement of mind which is the neceſſary conſequence of a long ſtate of ſlaviſh ſubjection, ſeems wholly to have ſuppreſſed the energy of ſpirit neceſſary to the undertaking of great and daring actions; and whilſt the inhabitants of thoſe Hindoo ſtates which, in the courſe of various revolutions, have preſerved or recovered their original independence, are enterpriſing and active, theſe, although acute and ingenious, are yet frigid and inert. Theſe imperfections do not prevent them, however, from being as induſtrious as the nature of the arts they purſue or the ſoil they cultivate renders neceſſary, at the ſame time that they make them the more eaſily governed; and they are accordingly uniformly ſubmiſſive and obedient.

From this it will appear that their inclinations and imbecilities lead them in general to prefer and purſue the quieter and more peaceable occupations of life; and, excepting the caſt of *Kyettries*, who are ſoldiers by birth or by the precepts of their religion, and who hire themſelves as mercenaries, indifferently, to any power under

under which they can procure employment, —they are almoſt all either manufacturers, or tillers of the ground. The few among them who acquire wealth, finding in *ſecrecy* their only ſecurity againſt *extortion*, never have their property ſo ſituated as would give them any intereſt in the fate of the country they inhabit; and, with reſpect to the remainder, if they be indulged in the unmoleſted exerciſe of their religious ceremonies, and the current proviſion of a ſlender maintenance for their families, they little care under what government they live, or by maſters of what complection they may be ruled: one ſet of conquerors is driven out by another, and their aſſumed rights again uſurped by a third; whilſt the *Hindoos*, whoſe country is the object, and from whoſe labour and ingenuity that object derives its value, behold the conteſt with an indifference of which thoſe who have never had an opportunity of being acquainted with the utter *apathy* of their diſpoſitions can form no idea:—the victors, whoever they may be, find the ſame intereſt in cheriſhing and protecting thoſe innocent and uſeful ſubjects as had the vanquiſhed ;—thus the Hindoos, comparatively ſpeaking, ſuffer but little in ſuch convulſions ; and taking no part in the quarrel, are in a great meaſure ſcreened from a participation in its conſequences.

The Mahommedans, greatly as they muſt have accumulated in ſo many ages, do yet bear an infinitely ſmall proportion in point of number to the Hindoos, among whom ſtrict temperance, and early marriage being indiſpenſable religious obſervances, population ſhoots with a vigour unknown in any other climate of equal temperature.

The purſuits of the Mahommedans, in general, differ very much from thoſe of the Hindoos.—Excepting their prieſts, lawyers, and other diſtinctions of the learned and recluſe, their views do almoſt univerſally lie in the army or the court ; ſome few, indeed, of the very loweſt ſort are traders or mechanicks, manufacturers or labourers.

The only Hindoos of any note are the *Zimeendars* or principal landholders, who are, however, totally dependent upon their Muſſulman lords, and anſwerable to them for the amount of their rents, or for a fixed tribute at which they are aſſeſſed, (beſides being obliged to aſſiſt them with ſuch proportion in men or money as may be required upon every emergency,)—ſo that the whole of the revenues ultimately centers with the Mahommedans, who fill all the important offices both in the army and in the other different departments of the ſtate, thereby reſerving the efficient power altogether in their own hands.

Thus it appears that, in theſe provinces, the great body of the people is compoſed of *Hindoos*, who till the ground or carry on the manufactures, and are invariably attached to the ſoil; whilſt the comparatively trifling number of *Mahommedans* hold the ſtate in ſubjection, diſpoſe of its revenues, and are removable by every change in politicks or power.

So long as the ſupreme government retained a vigour which was imparted to all its ſubordinate dependencies, the Hindoos in theſe provinces enjoyed, perhaps, as high a degree of happineſs and eaſe as could be conſiſtent with a ſtate of abſolute vaſſalage.—Whilſt the Houſe of Timour continued to flouriſh, the ear of the Emperor was always open to the complaints of the meaneſt of his ſubjects; an unremitting vigilance was preſerved over the conduct of all who were entruſted with authority; and the fatal conſequences of miſconduct or malverſation were known (in the prompt deciſions of abſolute power) to be equally rapid and unavoidable. Moreover, the Muſſulmans were not, like other foreigners who viſit Hindoſtan, mere *temporary ſojourners*. Obtaining entry into, or dominion over, a territory, their firſt deſigns,

originating

originating in the bigotry of a miſtaken zeal, or the barbarous rapacity of deſultory incurſion, were ſucceeded by the milder and more equitable views of a permanent eſtabliſhment, ſecured upon the principles of juſtice and moderation, which alone could render their acquiſitions capable of yielding them any laſting advantage:—they *ſettled* in the country, and thus becoming naturalized, had a certain intereſt in the ſoil.—The ſtern and harſh features of the Muſſulman character inſenſibly acquired ſome ſofter tints from an aſſociation with the mild, forbearing, and amiable temper of the Hindoos; and a ſtrong and united ſyſtem of adminiſtration afforded the latter protection, at once, from domeſtic oppreſſion and external injury.—This pleaſing face of things has, however, long ſince undergone a moſt deplorable alteration:——the power of one univerſal deſpot being overthrown, a way was opened for the intolerable and uncontrouled licentiouſneſs of numberleſs petty tyrants:—in the anarchy which increaſed with the increaſ-

ing

ing weakneſs of the Imperial Court, the violent and unprincipled factions of contending nobles united to tread all order and ſubordination under foot; and the tumultuous diſtractions hereby engendered extending to the more diſtant provinces, diffuſed their fatal effects whereſoever the royal authority had reached, at the ſame time that the licentiouſneſs of manners which is the uſual attendant of civil diſcord, introduced, perhaps, no ſmall change into the general character and deportment of the Muſſulmans about this period; and thus, from the operation of a variety of cauſes, they became equally diſſolute and rapacious.—In the rapid lapſe of revolutions, effected leſs frequently by the mandate of the prince than by the dagger of the hired aſſaſſin, all who could obtain truſt or command were anxious to ſeize the opportunity for making the moſt of ſituations ſo precarious:—as money was the life of every intrigue by which individuals hoped to riſe to power or ſcreen themſelves from injury, ſo no means, however nefarious,

were

were omitted to acquire it: all regard to the intereſt of the country or the proſperity of its inhabitants was loſt, where the verſatile ſituation of affairs was occaſioning a continual change of maſters:—and the Muſſulman Government every where degenerated into a confirmed ſyſtem of the moſt profligate venality and the moſt abandoned peculation; whilſt the great body of the people, deſtitute of any effectual patronage or protection, became by turns the prey of every upſtart adventurer, whoſe circumſtances or abilities enabled him to aſpire at rule: and it was, doubtleſs, the ſingular ſtate of theſe countries in the particulars we have deſcribed, which could have alone preſerved them from being altogether depopulated and laid waſte, in the progreſs of ſuch a ſcene of contention and bloodſhed.

Such was the actual ſtate of theſe provinces, when the folly and cruelty of Sujar-al-Dowlah, in its conſequences, formed a neceſſity for the Engliſh to act an important and deciſive part upon this theatre:—

theatre:—ſuch was the real ſtate of the territory which had been wreſted from the Mogul government by the Rohilla Afgans, when the policy (whether juſtifiable or otherwiſe) of ſecuring the dominions and ſupporting the cauſe of our ally induced the British government in Bengal to aſſiſt him in their expulſion.

The deductions to be drawn from theſe obſervations, ſo far as they may apply to the matter contained in the following pages, we ſhall leave to the judgement of the reader.

ADVERTISEMENT.

THE writer has ſtudiouſly endeavoured in the courſe of this work, as much as poſſible to avoid the repetition of Oriental terms and phraſes in their original form, which local knowledge alone can render clear and familiar to the European reader, and to ſubſtitute ſuch Engliſh expreſſions as bear the moſt appoſite ſignifications to them. But, with reſpect to *proper names* and *titles*, which ſo frequently occur, and can neither be omitted nor altered, and of which it is in general very difficult to retain a diſcriminating remembrance, he has followed a plan not heretofore adopted by any writer on thoſe ſubjects, and here begs leave to ſubjoin a liſt of the principal perſonages concerned or mentioned in the courſe of the following narrative, which may ſerve as a table of occaſional reference, in the peruſal of it.

The

The narrative begins by a retroſpect to the uſurpation of *Shere Shah.*

The ſubſtance of the hiſtory is included within the reigns of

Mahummed Shah Ahmed Shah Allumgeer II.	Mogul Emperors of Hindoſtan, and

Shah Aulum, the preſent Emperor.

Kummir-ad-deen-Khan, Vizier under Mahummed Shah.

Sefdar Jung, Vizier under Ahmed Shah.

Ghazee-ad-deen Khan, Prime Miniſter under Allumgeer II. not officially Vizier.

Sujar-al-Dowlah, Vizier under Shah Aulum.

Nadir Shah, King of Perſia.

Ahmed Abdâllee, Sovereign of Candahâr.

Genealogical

Genealogical Table *of the Family of* Allee Mahummed, Founder of the ROHILLA Government.

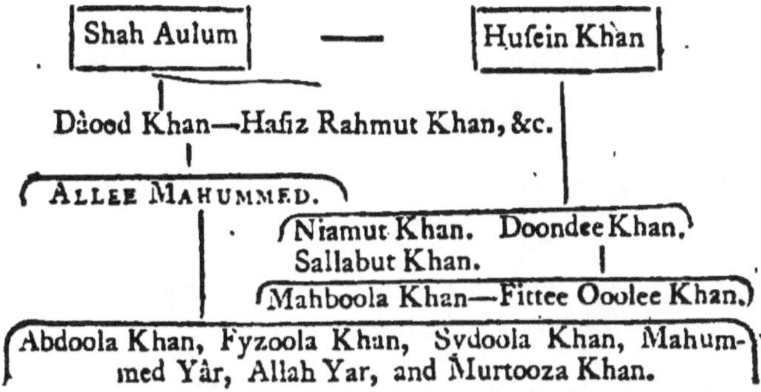

Offices in Rohilcund, *after the death of* Allee Mahummed.

Hafiz Rahmut
Doondee Khan } Guardians.

Niamut Khan
Sillâbut Khan } Assistant Ministers.

Futteh Khan, *Khansaman*, or Steward, (succeeded by his Son Ahmed Khan.

Sirdar Khan, *Buxy*, or Paymaster, (succeeded by his Son Ahmed Khan.

Other

Other Perſons of note.

Meer Munnoo, Son to the Vizier Kummir-ad-deen Khan, ſome time Commander in Chief of the Mogul Army.

Nejeeb al Dowlah, an Afgan of eminence, who acted as Miniſter at Delhi in the abſence of the preſent Emperor.

Zabita Khan, his Son.

Kaeem Jung, Chief of the Bungiſh tribe of Afgans, poſſeſſed of Ferrochabad.

Ahmed Khan Bungiſh, Brother and Succeſſor to Kaeem Jung.

Muzziffer Jung, Son and Succeſſor to Ahmed Khan Bungiſh.

&c.

A RELATION

A RELATION OF THE Origin, Progreſs, and Diſſolution, OF THE Government of the ROHILLA AFGANS, &c.

THE *Afgan Tartars* whoſe numerous tribes (under the general denomination of PATANS) occupy all the mountainous country which forms the North-weſtern boundary of Hindoſtan, had for a long ſeries of time held the greateſt part of this immenſe dominion in ſubjection, and furniſhed a race of monarchs who filled the imperial throne at Delhi upwards of three centuries, until the ſubjugation of the northern

India, and the overthrow of the Patân government, by the arms of Timur Beg.

About one hundred and forty years after that event, the usurpation of Mahummed Fereed-Shere-Shah, who in the nine hundred and fiftieth year of the Higera succeeded in his rebellion against the Emperor Humaioon, and drove that monarch into exile, having occasioned a violent distraction throughout all the countries in the neighbourhood of the capital, many of the inhabitants forsook those districts, and fled to the more distant provinces, hoping in the remoteness of their situations to find a security from the extortions of the usurper.

Shere Shah was himself an *Afgan* or *Patan*; and it was at this period that numbers of Afgans, expecting in him and his successors to see another Dynasty of the Patâns established upon the throne of Delhi, hastened from all parts to enlist under the standard of the new emperor.

As

As thoſe who fled from the tyrannical exactions of the uſurper and his creatures chiefly conſiſted of ſuch as had ſerved in the great offices of the ſtate, or as collectors of diſtricts and principal landholders under the former government, to ſome of theſe new comers he preſented grants of the evacuated eſtates and employments; many he raiſed to poſts of the higheſt power and diſtinction, and to all he gave every poſſible encouragement to ſettle in that part of Hindoſtan; and hence, on the death of Shere, when Humaioon recovered the empire by the defeat of Secunder, the nephew and ſucceſſor of his former competitor, the Afgans formed a powerful body in thoſe diſtricts.

As the inſurrections and rebellions which have at all times diſturbed the tranquillity of the Mogul government, preſented the moſt ample field of advancement and diſtinction to theſe bold and hardy ſoldiers of fortune, after the foregoing event, every adventurer who could collect a band of lawlefs freebooters, ufed to repair to Delhi to offe rhis fervices to the king; and, as the appointment of ftrangers, deftitute of any dangerous interefts or connexions, was the moft elligible policy in the government of the more diftant provinces, thefe offers were generally excepted; this wife precaution, however, which for a time certainly contributed to fupport the authority of the Mogul princes, and to preferve their empire entire, tended, in its unavoidable confequences, to precipitate their downfal; as the influence, credit, and numbers of thefe adventurers and their defcendants at length increafed to fuch a degree, as finally enabled them, in the general difmemberment of this unwieldy monarchy, to fecure to themfelves the independent poffeffion of many of its richeft provinces.

Of the various petty independencies which thus grew out of the ruins of the Mogul monarchy, one of the laft (though not the moft inconfiderable either in power or extent) was eftablifhed in the country of *Kuttaher*, in latter times better known by the name of *Rohilcund*.

This territory is ſituated to the eaſtward of the Ganges, between the province of Owde, and the firſt range of northern hills commonly called the *Cummou Mountains* ;—as its ſhape is nearly that of an irregular triangle, embraced on two of its ſides by the Ganges and the laſt-mentioned boundary, it would not be eaſy to give, in general terms, any accurate idea of its dimenſions ;—its mean length, however, is about one hundred and eighty, and its greateſt breadth about ninety miles, from which dimenſion it gradually decreaſes until it terminates in its moſt northern point at *Hirdewar*, where the Ganges flows through the before-mentioned range.

From a concurrence of happy circumſtances, (as it lies in a temperate climate, and is watered by ſeveral fine rivers) the country is, in general, rich and fertile, and contains many cities of conſiderable note, the chief of which are Owlah, Barilla, Moradabad, and Rampore. All theſe, previous to the uſurpations of the Rohillas, had been the capitals of royal *Fowjedarrys* (or lieutenancies) and the two former have ſince, at different times, reſpectively become the ſeat of government, during the ſhort period of Rohilla independence.

Among other Afgans who, from the cauſes already related, came to ſeek their fortunes in the lower countries, in the 1084th year of the Higera, (A. C. 1673) two brothers named Shah Aulum and Huſſein Khan, having forſaken their native mountains, ſettled in Kuttaher, where they procured ſome ſmall employments under the officers of the Mogul goverment; but nothing farther is related of them worthy of note.

Huſſein had three ſons; Doondy Khan, Niâmut Khan, and Sillaubet Khan; the firſt of whom will make a conſpicuous figure in the ſequel.—The elder brother, (Shah Aulum)

lum) had two ſons,—the firſt named Dâood Khan, and the ſecond Rahmut Khan.

The latter of theſe not bearing any important part in the enſuing ſcene of action for ſeveral years, it is needleſs to obſerve more of him at preſent than that his firſt outſet in life was in a mercantile capacity, ſuitable to the obſcurity of his origin; and that he continued to trade between Lahore and Delhi, until he was called forth to fill more elevated and important ſtations.

Dâood choſe a military life; and after the manner of other Afgan adventurers, collecting together ſome followers, offered himſelf and was admitted as a volunteer into an army ſent by the vizier to oppoſe the incurſions of the Mahrattas, who about this period had acquired a conſiderable degree of power, and were become not a little formidable to the Mogul government, laying waſte the country between Narwa and Gowalior, and extending their depredations

 towards

towards the banks of the Jumna.——On this expedition Daood diſtinguiſhed himſelf by his bravery; and being on a particular occaſion, detached from the main army, had the addreſs to ſurprize and cut off a party of the enemy, bringing in with him ſome elephants and other ſpoils,

As a reward for this ſervice, Dâood, on the return of the royal forces, obtained a grant of a little diſtrict in the territory of Budâvon, which forms a part of Rohilcund; but, a retired life ill ſuiting with his active and enterpriſing ſpirit, he preſently recruited his little force, conſiſting of the firſt followers of his fortune, with a conſiderable body of his countrymen, and with theſe rendered many ſervices to the neighbouring Rajahs and Zimeendârs, who were happy to procure his ſupport in their frequent diſputes with each other, which in thoſe countries are generally decided by force.

The fame of this bold partizan ſoon reached

reached the ears of the Rajah of *Cummou* (or *Kummâoon*) who invited Dâood into his ſervice, and in a little time after gave him the command of all his forces;—in this ſituation Dâood performed many ſervices of conſiderable advantage to his maſter; not meeting however with thoſe rewards to which he thought his merits and ſervices entitled him, he was preparing to leave the Rajah's employ in diſguſt; but in attempting to effect this he was ſeized; and the Rajah cruelly ordered his feet to be cut off, and the ſinews of his legs to be forcibly drawn out from the ſtumps; an operation which ſoon cauſed the parts to mortify, and occaſioned his death.

Dâood left two ſons; Mahummed, and Allee Mahummed*:—of the former of

 theſe

* Some accounts have ſaid that Allee Mahummed was *not* the *ſon* of Dâood, but by birth a *Hindoo*, and adopted by him:—this however is not only an incongruity (as a Hindoo is ſeldom nor ever known to be adopted by a Muſſulman,) but is moreover altogether unſupported

theſe nothing remarkable is recorded ;—but it was to the aſpiring abilities and intrepid perſeverance of the latter, (co-operating with the turbulence of the times) that the Afgans owed the foundation of their independance in Rohilcund.

Dâood had always indulged a ſtrong partiality in favour of his younger ſon Allee Mahummed, and had him early inſtructed in every military exerciſe, and in all other accompliſhments which might enable him to make an eminent and ſucceſsful figure in the execution of that plan of ſeparate and uncontrolled independence which the increaſing imbecility of the Imperial authority had taught him to hope might ſome time or other, with the aſſiſtance of his countrymen, be effected in Rohilcund.

---

unſupported in the original Perſian manuſcript, where he is poſitively mentioned as Dâood's ſecond ſon.——Of the other ſon (Mahummed) the MS. takes no farther notice whatſoever, except merely mentioning his name, as above.

When

When Dâood firſt conceived his deſign of quitting the Rajah of Cummou's ſervice, he took care previouſly to tranſmit the principal part of his property, under the charge of his favourite ſon, to Budâvon; ſo that, upon his death, Allee Mahummed found himſelf at once poſſeſſed of conſiderable wealth, and ſupported by a numerous train of his father's adherents, to whom his gallant and munificent ſpirit had much endeared him, and whoſe deſperate circumſtances and experienced bravery rendered them the fitteſt inſtruments for the proſecution of his ambitious views.

With theſe he entered into the ſervice of Azmut-Oolah Khan, a perſon of rank, who had been appointed from the court of Delhi Fowjdar * of Moradabad:—here he ſoon

* A Fowjdar implies, in its literal meaning, a commander of troops; and is an officer appointed to act as governor or lieutenant of a diſtrict, under a commiſſion from the king, which empowers him to levy troops and make war, &c. as occaſion may require.

ſoon ingratiated himſelf with Azmut-Oolah, ſo as to procure, through his means, a renewal of the grant which had been beſtowed on his father, and alſo to obtain the collection of a conſiderable purgunna on the part of the Emperor, together with a *Jeydad*, or conſignment of ſome villages, which he artfully procured for the ſupport of his followers.

Azmut Oolah being ſhortly after recalled to court, Allee Mahummed ſeized the opportunity which this interval afforded him, whilſt there was no royal deputy at hand who might control his motions or counteract his deſigns, to raiſe a ſtrong force, and eſtabliſh himſelf in the poſſeſſion of thoſe lands, the charge of which he had obtained through the favour of Azmut-bolah :—and as theſe parts of India have at all times ſwarmed with multitudes of vagrants (chiefly Afgans) who wander over the country in ſearch of employment, and are ready to enliſt under any ſtandard that may be raiſed, or to fight in any cauſe

that

that may offer, ſo he ſoon increaſed the number of his followers (which, at the time of his father's death had not exceeded *three hundred* in all) to ſuch a degree*, that when a ſucceſſor to Azmut-Oolah was appointed from Delhi, the Afgan found himſelf in a condition to make his own terms, and even to engage him (by ſome valuable preſents) ſo much in his favour as to procure, through his means, a commiſſion from the Court, authorizing him to retain the charge of the lands already mentioned; and alſo the gift of a ſmall Jageer in addition thereto, for the ſupport of his dignity.

Allee Mahummed thus raiſed to ſome degree of rank and conſequence, neglected

* It may, perhaps, appear ſurpiſing that an obſcure individual ſhould be able to collect or ſupport a formidable force with ſuch facility:—it is to be conſidered, however, that in an Indian army the comparative number of thoſe who receive regular pay is very ſmall: the horſe and accoutrements of every trooper are his own property, and he often engages with no other view than *plunder*.

no

no means in his power to ſtrengthen his intereſt and enlarged his connections, and the circumſtances of the times afforded him ample ſcope for accompliſhing theſe views by methods the moſt eaſy and obvious.—The Court of Delhi being, at this time, torn to pieces by the ſtruggles of contending nobles, had loſt much of its power and influence; ſo that Allee Mahummed, conſcious of his ſtrength, ſhewed little attention to the imperial mandates, and delayed or avoided, on various frivolous pretexts, any payment of revenue into the royal treaſury, employing the income of his lands in raiſing troops, purchaſing artillery and military ſtores, and, above all, in ſecuring the friendſhip of many of the principal perſonages in the preſence, by a judicious and well-timed liberality; neither was he remiſs in cultivating the attachment of the lower orders by the ſame practices as enabled him to ſucceed with their ſuperiors; and he now only waited an opportunity to throw off the maſk and openly aſſert his independance, as moſt of the

governors

governors in the more diſtant provinces had already done. Such a one preſently preſented itſelf, although perhaps ſomewhat prematurely.

Ômdat al Moolk, who was at this period *Meer Buchſhy* or Paymayſter-General of the Empire, and poſſeſſed a conſiderable ſhare of influence at court, held the diſtricts of Owlah and Minnownah in Jageer from the King.—Theſe diſtricts bordered cloſe upon the lands in the poſſeſſion of Allee Mahummed; and the paymaſter had diſpatched a favourite confidential ſervant to collect the rents: whether this perſon had received any particular inſtructions with regard to the Afgan is not certainly known; but, very ſoon after his arrival, he gave occaſion for a quarrel, by endeavouring to ſequeſter the rents of ſome villages to which Allee Mahummed laid claim, but which the deputy inſiſted lay within the bounds of his Maſter's Jageer.—An encroachment of this nature the high-ſpirited Afgan would by no means ſubmit to; and

and after various disputes, and ineffectual negotiations, the deputy resolved to attempt executing his designs by force; and, as his power was supported by the name and countenance of the royal authority, he vainly flattered himself that no troops would venture to oppose him:—the event shewed, however, how much he was mistaken in his conjecture, as, in an engagement that ensued he himself was slain, and his troops totally routed.

In this exploit Allee Mahummed strengthened himself with all the stores and numerous artillery of the enemy: but this was not the only advantage he derived from it; the boldness of his actions and munificence of his disposition had already acquired him some degree of credit with his countrymen, when the fame of this victory raised his character so high among them, that multitudes of Afgans immediately came from every part of the country to offer their services; and as he attached them strongly to his interest by making

over

ever to them almoſt the whole of the revenues of his diſtricts, thoſe vagrants ſoon became enthuſiaſts in his cauſe, and were ready to ſupport him in any attempt, however deſperate.

Nor was Allee Mahummed deſtitute of a powerful friend at court, to raiſe his character, and extenuate his oppoſition to the imperial authority: in truth, ſo miſerably was the Mogul government ſunk at this time into the baſeſt venality and corruption, that Rebellion itſelf could with eaſe *bribe* advocates to plead its cauſe; and where this means failed, the ſame effect was frequently produced in the outrageous animoſities of unprincipled and factious ambition.

The high office of the *Vizarèt* was, at this period, held by Kummir-ad-deen Khan, a nobleman of the firſt character for integrity and abilities:—It is probable, however, that the rectitude of his principles was not altogether proof of againſt the

E ſeductions

ſeductions of immediate intereſt; as Allee Mahummed, from the firſt riſe of his fortune, had paid court to him with unremitted aſſiduity, in the way we have already mentioned; and it is certain that the Vizier ſupported him on every occaſion, where decency and a regard for reputation would admit of his ſo doing, in the ſequel:—Neither was he, in the preſent inſtance, unaffected by thoſe other motives we have mentioned above; as a mutual enmity, originating in the jealouſy of court intrigue, had long ſubſiſted between him and the before-mentioned Omdat-al-Moolk.—Allee Mahummed, after his victory over the deputy of Omdat-al-Moolk, as already related, ſeized the latter's Jagheer, and converted the revenues ariſing from it to his own uſe: the paymaſter-general, already incenſed at the death of his ſervant, when he found that his eſtate was thus appropriated, made loud complaints of the iniquity of ſuch violent and flagitious proceedings:—but the Vizier, not reflecting how ſoon his *own* intereſts might ſuffer by the encroach-

encroachments of ſuch a daring uſurper, and happy in ſupporting any one in oppoſition to his rival, exerted the whole of his weight and authority at court in behalf of the Afgan Zimeendar, repreſenting his breach with the deputy as ariſing ſolely from the raſhneſs and rapacity of the latter, who, inſtead of attempting to effect the purpoſes for which he had been ſent, had endeavoured to rob Allee Mahummed of all his treaſure and effects, with a view to enrich himſelf with the ſpoil.—The raſhneſs of the deputy's proceedings certainly afforded ſome colour of juſtice to this plea; and although theſe arguments had been weaker, yet they would have ſufficed to turn the ſcale in Allee Mahummed's favour, when ſupported by the credit and influence of the Miniſter.

Another incident took place, ſhortly after this, which ſerved to give Allee Mahummed a reputation for loyalty, ſuch as his real deſigns but little entitled him to, and to confirm and increaſe the intereſt he had already laid the foundation of at court.

In the preſent diſtracted ſtate of the empire, every petty Zimeendar dared to riſe in rebellion againſt the government.—There was a ſettlement of *Seyds* of the tribe of *Barrah*, which had been eſtabliſhed ſome years before in the neighbourhood of *Anopſhéer* (a town oppoſite to Rohilcund, on the weſtern bank of the Ganges) where their leader or chief, Seyd-ad-deen, a man of a troubleſome and turbulent diſpoſition, had been admitted as a renter; and at length, in a confidence of his own ſtrength and the imbecility of the government, excited his followers to raiſe an inſurrection, and to murder all the Emperor's officers who were acting in that quarter, or to expel them from their diſtrict:—in the ſuppreſſion of this diſturbance Allee Mahummed (from whatever motive) eminently diſtinguiſhed himſelf, joining the Emperor's forces, and entirely routing the

the insurgents in an engagement in which their ring leader was killed.

It was generally supposed that Allee Mahummed had been induced to engage thus warmly in the royal cause, at the instigation of the Vizier; and in gratitude for the countenance and favour he had lately shewn him; however that might be, Kummir-ad-Deen did not fail to represent the gallantry and loyalty of his conduct on the late occasion in the most favourable light to the Emperor, who, as a reward, conferred upon the Afgan the dignity of an Ameer, with the title of a *Nawab*, accompanied by a *Khelaat*, or honorary dress; at the same time issuing a *Firman*, or royal warrant, confirming him in the lands which he had so surreptitiously possessed himself of, and investing him with other honours and ranks of distinction.

This sudden and extraordinary elevation of a man who had, on more than one occasion, manifested a disposition by no means conſiſtent with the imperial intereſt, was as impolitick and ſhort ſighted in the court as it was fortunate for Allee Mahummed, whoſe fame and conſequence were enhanced by it in a prodigious degree: but, in the moment when his fortune ſeemed to be ripening, he was again engaged in a buſineſs on which he riſqued all his intereſt and ſupport at Delhi.

Rajah Hir-Nund, a Hindoo of ſome eminence, was appointed by the Vizier to the *Fowjdarrey* of Moradabad.

As the Vizier, however friendly his diſpoſition might be, was well aware of the neceſſity of curbing and keeping within bounds the aſpiring ſpirit of the Afgan chief, the new Fowjdar had particular inſtructions to look narrowly into the conduct of Allee Mahummed, whoſe views had already begun to extend in conſequence of his late acceſſion of rank:—He was alſo directed to make requiſition of the proportion due to government from the

rents

rents of the Afgan's lands, which were comprehended within the jurifdiction of the Moradabad *Fowjdarrey*; and, to enable him to do fo with effect, he was accompanied by a confiderable body of horfe, and a refpectable train of artillery.

Hir-Nund, on his arrival at his government, intimated his defire of an interview with Allee Mahummed; this, however, (although an indifpenfable mark of duty and attention to the royal commiffion) the latter declined: the Rajah, foon after, made a formal demand of the royal quitrents, to which Allee Mahummed replied only by a repetition of fubterfuges and delays; and at the fame time began to collect his numerous followers, and to put himfelf in a pofture of defence.—The Rajah appears to have been fomewhat violent and precipitate: in fact, the recent honours beftowed upon the Afgan had excited the envy of many; and there were not wanting thofe who would endeavour, in hopes of effecting his ruin, to ftimulate the

the Fowjedar to adapt an abſolute and overbearing mode of conduct, tending to provoke rather than to intimidate:—At length preſumption on the one hand and diſguſt upon the other urged both parties to action:—the Fowjdar made ſome movements with his troops which ſeemed to indicate a deſign of ſeizing on a number of ſmall forts within the country of Allee Mahummed; but, if he had any ſuch intentions, they were fruſtrated by the valour and addreſs of his adverſary, who attacked the army of Hir Nund one morning by ſurpriſe, and gave them a total overthrow, ſeizing on all their treaſure, artillery, and camp equipage;—and the body of the unfortunate Rajah was found, after the engagement, in his tent, ſtabbed in ſeveral places; ſo that it was ſtrongly ſuſpected he had periſhed by ſome colluſive treachery.

Allee Mahummed immediately made a repreſentation of the nature of this rupture to the Vizier, and endeavoured to diſcharge himſelf of any blame in the tranſaction, as having been in ſome meaſure compelled to exert his means of defence in the manner he had done by the headſtrong violence of Hir-Nund.—The Vizier, however, was by no means pleaſed with the buſineſs, in which he had been conſiderably injured in his own property, as the greateſt part of the artillery and ſtores belonged to him;—and he alſo reſented the death of the Rajah, who was an old confidential ſervant, and his particular favourite.—He therefore diſpatched his ſon, Meer Munnoo, with a conſiderable force, to demand ſatisfaction for the injury which the imperial authority had ſuſtained in the diſcomfiture of the Fowjdar.

The remainder of this tranſaction is involved in ſome obſcurity.—We ſhall not, however, hazard any conjectures, but ſhall ſimply adhere, in our relation of it, to the account as it ſtands in the original.

Meer Munno proceeded with his troops to Secunderabâd, and from thence to the banks

banks of the Ganges opposite to Daranágûrr, at which place the river is fordable in the dry season, but by a long winding passage, insomuch that it would be very difficult for any army to cross over there in that manner if opposed by an enemy ;—here he saw the Afgan chief encamped on the opposite shore, with a force so much superior to his own, that he did not judge it prudent to attempt the passage.——In this situation the armies lay in sight of each other for some time, 'till at length the two commanders came to a proper understanding, and a negociation took place, in the course of which Allee Mahummed found means not only to make his peace, but also greatly to reinforce his interest with the Vizier by bestowing a daughter in marriage upon one of the sons of that minister *with a considerable dowry*; and (probably in consequence of this politick measure) procured a grant of the lands formerly occupied by Hir-Nund, which he henceforth included within the circle of his possessions, and out of which he engaged to pay a stipulated annual quit-

rent

rent into the royal treaſury.—As Allee Mahummed, and the greateſt part of the followers by whoſe aſſiſtance he had been enabled to riſe, were of the tribe of Afgans denominated *Rohees*, or *Rohillas*, (ſo termed from *Roh*, which in the Pâtan dialect ſignifies *a mountainous country*,) it was about this period that the diſtrict of Kuttâher began to be diſtinguiſhed by the name of *Rohilcund**, although this term was not applied to it in any publick inſtruments or other authentick records until ſome years after.

Allee Mahummed having thus laid the foundation of independence in Rohilcund, reſolved to uſe the preſent interval of tranquillity, not only to eſtabliſh himſelf in his new acquiſitions, but to revenge the death of his father Dâood, by attacking the Rajah of *Kummâoon*.

The diſtrict of *Kummâoon* (or *Cummów*)

---

* *Anglicé*—"The *place* or *reſidence* of the *Rohillas*."

lies

lies along the back of thoſe hills which derive their name from it, and which form the northern boundary of the low country to the eaſtward of the Ganges.—It does not appear that it ever had been before ſubdued by the Muſſulmans, although the Rajah paid a ſmall tribute and acknowledged fealty to the Mogul government.——Preparatory to this expedition, Allee Mahummed ſettled the interior policy of his country, and put his finances under proper regulations. He then advanced towards the hills with a body of fifteen thouſand veteran Afgans. He was joined in the beginning of his march by a multitude of predatory vagabonds, who abound in every part of Hindoſtan, and are ready to join in any excurſion merely with a view to ſhare in the plunder; but they receive no pay, and are of no uſe in action.—As Allee Mahummed was ſenſible of the difficulties he would have to ſtruggle with in the courſe of his undertaking, eſpecially with reſpect to proviſions, he determined to throw off the in-

cumbrance

cumbrance of thoſe uſeleſs banditti, and accordingly publiſhed a proclamation declaring "that any ſtranger or other perſon not enrolled, who ſhould be found within the camp after a certain day, ſhould be puniſhed with death."--The rigorous execution of this menace in a few inſtances ſoon drove away all ſuperfluous mouths, and eventually contributed not a little to the ſucceſs of the expedition.—Allee Mahummed now proceeded to Coſipore, a fortreſs on the borders of the northern Foreſts which fringe the ſkirts of the Cummow hills to the depth of ſeveral miles;—here he collected a large ſtock of proviſions, and alſo carriages for as much grain and other neceſſaries as would ſerve his little army for two months. —Theſe meaſures, indiſpenſably requiſite to the ultimate ſucceſs of the Afgans, neceſſarily occaſioned ſome delay; ſo that the Rajah was ſufficiently aware of the Rohilla chief's intentions, and prepared for his reception by fortifying all the ghautts or paſſes over the mountains which

led

led into his country.—Allee Mahummed had, ſome time before, employed his ſcouts to explore the woody region which (as above obſerved) runs along the foot of the Cummow hills, in hopes of being able to avoid the Rajah by purſuing an unexpected route.—Some of theſe meſſengers returned with an account of their having diſcovered a practicable paſſage by which (although their deſcription of it was by no means encouraging) it was determined to advance.——The Afgans, accordingly, boldly penetrated at once through the foreſts, and after a march of eighteen days, during which they ſuffered incredible hardſhips and fatigues, at length gained the upper country, and arrived at *Chumnáwtee*, (a village in *Kummáoon*) which was the firſt inhabited place they had ſeen for ſome time paſt.—The troops of Allee Mahummed here found themſelves reduced to act under every diſadvantage, as they had no proviſions but what they brought upon their backs, and had been obliged to abandon their artillery, and alſo to leave all their

their horſes and other cattle behind, theſe being unable to ſurmount the ſteeps; the ſucceſs of this bold attempt, however, ſo terrified the Rajah, that he never offered to oppoſe the Afgan troops, but fled his dominion, and took refuge in the neighbouring country of Sirnagur.—Allee Mahummed thus making himſelf maſter of the territory without reſiſtance, ſoon overran it, and acquired a prodigious booty; and having rented the whole diſtrict of *Kummâoon* to the Rajah of Sirnagurr for three lacks per annum, he returned with his plunder to Owlah.

The fortunate reſult of this expedition, and the riches which Allee Mahummed and his followers had acquired by it, would not a little have contributed to the extenſion and confirmation of his power in Rohilcund;—but ſoon after his arrival at Owlah, he found himſelf once more involved in a quarrel with the court, out of which he did not extricate himſelf with his uſual ſucceſs.

Some of the Afgan chief's Rohilla retainers had a dispute with the servants of Sefdar Jung, Subadar of Owde; who had been sent by their master to cut *Saal** timbers; which abound in the forests at the back of Kuttaher :---this produced a fray, in which several were killed on both sides; and the gumashté (or *agent*) who commanded Sefdar Jung's people, was obliged to fly, leaving behind him all his effects, which, according to their usual custom, were seized as lawful spoil by the Rohillas.

The agent repaired immediately to Owde, and laid a complaint before the Subadar, who, incensed at the treatment his servant had met with, and considering his own honour concerned to resent it, repaired immediately to Delhi, and represented to the sovereign (Mahummed Shah)

* The *Saal* is a very beautiful tree, growing perfectly strait, to the height of 60 or 70 feet; of considerable use in building, &c.

the injurious inſult he had ſuſtained in ſuch ſtrong colours, that an order was immediately diſpatched to Allee Mahummed, directing him to recover and reſtore all the Gumaſhté's effects; with ſtrict injunctions to deliver up ſuch of the Rohillas as had been concerned in the before-mentioned diſturbance.

To this requiſition Allee Mahummed returned an anſwer filled with expreſſions of the moſt ſubmiſſive obedience,—but, at the ſame time intimating—"that he "would never ſuffer the Gumaſhtés of "any man to come into his country with- "out his conſent; that he could not but "approve of what his people had done; "and that he would neither reſtore the "effects nor deliver up the plunderers, "who had received, in the inſolence of "the Subadar's people, a provocation "which ſufficiently juſtified their pro- "ceedings."

This incautious reply, which amounted

to

to an explicit declaration of avowed rebellion, at length roused the court from the supine lethargy into which it had been so long lulled, with respect to the designs of Allee Mahummed; and the Emperor having at present no other object of greater moment to occupy his attention, resolved, if possible, to root out* the Afgan freebooters, and expel them entirely from Kuttâher. Sefdar Jung, who hoped by the disgrace and overthrow of Allee Mahummed to add Rohilcund to the extensive dominion he already held, which from its relative situation would render the whole of his possessions perfectly compact and easily defensible, was induced by every motive of interest, as well as of revenge, to enter warmly into this determination,

* The term, in the original is *isteesál*, the casual interpretation of which (upon another occasion) into "*extirpate*," has given rise to great and unfounded clamour:—the *true* meaning is here exhibited, both in the *translation* of it, and in the circumstance to which it applies.

and

and to ſupport and urge it to the Emperor by every argument in his power. He repreſented the notorious turbulence and rapacity of the Afgans, and the contumacious demeanour of Allee Mahummed, which had been ſufficiently diſplayed, not only in his withholding the revenues of the country with the charge of which he had been entruſted, but alſo in his lately undertaking a predatory expedition againſt the Rajah of *Kummâoon* without pretext or authority;—and the diſgrace to the imperial honour, in ſuffering a contemptible tribe of fifteen or twenty thouſand lawleſs adventurers to exerciſe abſolute ſway over a territory of ſuch value and extent as *Kuttâber*, under the immediate eye of the court, and almoſt, as it were, within ſight of the royal reſidence. The Subadar alſo endeavoured to engage the Vizier, Kummir-ad-deen, to take a deciſive part in the meaſures he propoſed; but that Miniſter, from a jealouſy of the growing influence of Sefdar Jung, although the circumſtances of the times obliged him to exhibit an appearance of coinciding with him, yet endeavoured in ſecret to thwart and counteract his views ;—this underhand oppoſition on the part of the Vizier, however, was not ſufficient to ſcoth the Shah's reſentment, or to prevent the proſecution of his deſign.

Although the treaſury was, at this period, very low, yet, by the aſſiſtance of Sefdar Jung and ſome other nobles who hoped to ſhare in the fruits of Allee Mahummed's ruin, the Emperor was enabled to levy a conſiderable army, at the head of which he marched towards Rohilcund in the month *Ribbee-al-Sanee*, A. H. 1154. *

Allee Mahummed does not ſeem to have acted on this occaſion with his uſual promptitude and capacity : whether he might hope, by not attempting any reſiſtance, to have the affair made up through the interpoſition of the Vizier ;—whether he expected that the violent feuds among

* A. C. 1743.

the

the king's miniſters might operate to his advantage,—or was doubtful of the fidelity of his own people;—whatever was his motive, he never attempted to face the royal forces; they croſſed the Ganges at Rangout without oppoſition; and proclamations were forthwith iſſued throughout the neighbouring country offering protection and reward to all ſuch as ſhould deſert Allee Mahummed, and threatened his retainers with the ſevereſt puniſhments.—Sefdar Jung ſeconded the force of theſe edicts by a variety of underhand practices, of which his long experience in the ſchool of crooked politics had rendered him a very complete maſter; and, by means of numerous emiſſaries, ſpread terror and diſaffection throughout the troops of Allee Mahummed; ſo that he found himſelf in a ſhort time almoſt entirely deſerted; and to avoid immediate deſtruction, was under the neceſſity of taking refuge, with a few followers who ſtill remained faithful to him, in the fort of *Bangûr*, which was immediately inveſted and cloſely beſieged by the royal army.—Here, when ſeemingly on the brink of inevitable ruin, his affairs were ſuddenly retrieved by the mediation of the Vizier and ſome other Amras, who, in oppoſition to the Subadar of Owde (whom they all feared and deteſted) joined in prevailing upon Mahummed Shah to be reconciled to the Afgan chief.—He was accordingly permitted to approach the preſence and make his peace, on condition of relinquiſhing his country and attending the King to Delhi. In conſequence of this compromiſe, Allee Mahummed and his garriſon ſurrendered and were honourably treated, notwithſtanding the remonſtrances of Sefdar Jung, who inſiſted on the expediency of making an example of the contumacious Afgan.—But the Emperor's lenity was not the only diſappointment the Subadar experienced on the preſent occaſion, as he failed in his deſign of getting charge of *Kuttáher*, which, to his uſpeakable mortification, was entruſted to the government of Feridad-deen Khan, the ſon of Azmut-Ooolih, formerly Fowjdâr of Moradabad.

Allee

Allee Mahummed, on his attending the Emperor to Delhi, left his family and moſt valuable effects at Budâvon, on the borders of his late poſſeſſions, where he hoped he might, ſome time or other, be able to reinſtate himſelf.

Sefdar Jung, provoked at the unprofitable event of the late expedition, and apprehenſive that ſome future coincidence of circumſtances, by reſtoring Allee Mahummed to his lands, might ſubvert the hopes he ſtill entertained of adding that tract to the province of Oude, omitted no means by which he might effect the Afgan's ruin; and ſuch ſway did he bear in the councils of the King, that Allee Mahummed found it expedient to ſecrete himſelf on one occaſion, in order to avoid the effects of his malice.

In warding off the blows aimed at him by the inſiduous and implacable Subadar, Allee Mahummed found himſelf much aſſiſted by ſome of the principal nobles who had before interceded for him at Bangûr, not more perhaps out of regard to him than from hatred to his enemy; and (as it was deemed proper to keep him for some time in a kind of honourable restraint) the Vizier gave him apartments in his palace, in which he remained confined as a sort of *state prisoner* for several months. In the mean time, in order to avoid any disturbances which might be excited in favour of the Afgan chief, a *Firman* was issued, prohibiting Rohillas, and all other Patâns, of every description, who had formerly acted under Allee Mahummed from crossing the Ganges, or entering Delhi, under any pretence whatsoever.

The only step, however, which could have effectually broken the Afgan confederacy, had been neglected.—When Allee Mahummed surrendered, no precautions were taken for the expulsion of his friends and retainers from *Kuttáher*, (as had been intended,) hence they still continued to hold a local consequence and strength; and shortly

ſhortly after the Emperor's return to Delhi, a conſiderable number of them collected at Sumbull (a city in the northern Rohilcund)—and becoming impatient of the abſence of their popular and ſucceſsful chief, and perhaps aſhamed of their late puſillanimous deſertion of him, reſolved to make an effort to releaſe him from his preſent confinement, and ſet him again at their head. For this purpoſe upwards of four thouſand of them, by the connivance of ſome Afgan commanders in the royal forces, eluding the vigilance of the guards at the fords, croſſed the Ganges, and paſſing over the *Doâb* * province in ſeparate parties under different diſguiſes, aſſembled at a garden or villa in the ſuburbs of Delhi, from whence they iſſued in a body to the royal palace, and there, with much clamour, inſiſted on the enlargement of Allee Mahummed. There was at this time but a

* This, (as the name ſignifies) is the country lying between *two rivers*, the Ganges and the Jumna; Delhi is ſituated upon the latter.

very ſmall force in Delhi ; a conſiderable part of thoſe lately levied had been already diſbanded ; ſome had been left under the command of Ferid-ad-deen, to ſecure the tranquillity of the countries beyond the Ganges ; and the remainder had, a little time before, marched under Meer Munnoo, towards Lahore*, as there was an apprehenſion of the empire being attacked from that quarter :—thus ſituated, the court was not a little ſtartled at this unexpected and alarming inſurrection ; and their ignorance of its origin and extent increaſed the terror and perplexity of the King and his miniſters.—There were, however, among the latter, ſome Afgan *Amras*, who were in ſecret not much diſpleaſed at this ſedition, and they determined to make uſe of it as an argument for the immediate releaſe of Allee Mahummed, whoſe enterpriſing abilities they conceived might contribute to the aggrandizement of their party : they therefore urged the neceſſity of taking ſome ſtep in his favour, in order to avert the gathering ſtorm ; becauſe, being exceedingly

* Page 29.

exceedingly popular with his countrymen, there was reaſon to apprehend that the preſent tumult might extend to a general inſurrection of all the *Patâns* in the northern provinces, which, in the imbecile condition the ſtate was then reduced to, might be attended with the moſt ſerious conſequences.

The unhappy neceſſity of preſent circumſtances gave ſuch weight to theſe arguments as at length induced the miniſters to yield to the turbulent clamours of Allee Mahummed's adherents; and the Vizier found himſelf conſtrained reluctantly to give way to the tide of general opinion;—for, though from family connection, and other conſiderations, he was much the Afgan's friend, yet he by no means conſidered him a perſon fit to be entruſted at any diſtance from the immediate eye of government.

It would have been dangerous, in the preſent criſis, to ſuffer Allee Mahummed to return to his former possessions;—the collection of the country of Sirhind was therefore bestowed upon him, where, being at a distance from his original connections, it was presumed he would remain more amenable to the authority of the court:—Allee Mahummed accordingly proceeded to that place, leaving two of his children with the Vizier as hostages for his fidelity.

Allee Mahummed had, at this period, six sons,—Abdoola Khan, Fyzoola Khan, Sydoola Khan, Mahummed Yar Khan, Allah Yar Khan, and Murtooza Khan;—of these, the *first* and *second* were the pledges delivered as above.

It was shortly after the appointment of Allee Mahummed to Sirhind that the famous *Ahmed Shah Abdallee* invaded Hindostan.*

No notice has been taken, in its proper place, of the invasion of Nadir Shah, as that event did not, at the time, bear any

* A.H. 1155, A.C. 1744.

direct

direct relation to the hiſtory of the Afgans;—but as its deſtructive conſequences to the Mogul power contributed not a little to the facility of forming the Rohilla, and many other independent eſtabliſhments which ſoon after ſprung up in different parts of India, and, though not in its immediate operation, yet in its ſubſequent effects, materially tended to alter the general ſyſtem, it may here be neceſſary to take a ſhort retroſpect, as a proper introduction to what follows.

——— Nadir Shah, after ſubjugating all the provinces of Perſia, and ſpreading his ravages over the region which formed the ancient empire of Ghizni, advanced into Candahar, from whence he was induced, by the factions which weakened and diſtracted the Mogul government, to proceed towards Delhi;—and to this ſtep he was, moreover, invited by ſome malcontent Amras in India, who expected in the ruin of their monarch, and the overthrow of the ſtate, to find opportunities for

the

the gratification of their own flagitious ambition.

It was not probable that a weak and effeminate prince, aided (or rather *governea)* by a council composed (the Vizier only excepted) of men of the most abandoned principles, each of whom was solely occupied in the care of his own little interests, without the smallest attention to or regard for the publick good, should be able to conduct an army so as to make an effectual stand against the incursion of troops who had been bred up in war, and were long accustomed to victory:—after an action in which, however, it appears that the Moguls behaved in a manner not altogether unworthy of their ancient character, some of the principal commanders in Mahummed Shah's army, perceiving that the irregular efforts of personal bravery would, in the end, prove no match for the undaunted firmness of Nadir's disciplined veterans, began to despair; whilst those traitors who had invited the Persian to invade their country, and among whom were

were ſome of the chief ſervants of the Emperor, ſecretly commenced ſeparate negociations with the enemy;—and intelligence of this being conveyed io Mahummed Shah, the unhappy prince, tottering on the brink of ruin in the midſt of his irreſolute officers and perfidious miniſters, was adviſed by his Vizier to throw himſelf upon the mercy and generoſity of his adverſary. He accordingly ſurrendered, and was treated with reſpect; and the Perſian forces proceeded towards Delhi, which city Nadir Shah entered upon the ninth of March, A. D. 1739.

The particulars which followed have been minutely related by others: it is therefore ſufficient to obſerve that having, by the ſeizure of the royal treaſury and regalia, by contributions, taxes, and pillages, collected to the enormous value of *ſeventy millions ſterling*, Nadir Shah returned towards Perſia, marking his route with horror and devaſtation. Not very long after, he was aſſaſſinated; upon which event, a number

of

of rivals immediately ſtarted up to diſpute the ſucceſſion to his extenſive conqueſts, and, as is always the caſe on ſuch occaſions, that empire which he had formed with ſo much riſque and labour, and ſuch deſtruction to the human race, fell to pieces, and became divided into a number of independent ſovereignties.

Among other adventurers who raiſed themſelves to royalty upon this occaſion was Ahmed Khan, ſurnamed *Abdállee.*

Ahmed Khan was an Afgan, a native of Herat, of the tribe of Afgans denominated *Dúran Abdâl*, whoſe anceſtors had held a conſiderable dominion in the mountains which ſeparate Hindoſtan from Perſia:—the fortunes of his family being ruined, and his country overrun by the arms of Nadir Shah, he was conſtrained to enter into the ſervice of the Perſian; and although at firſt entertained in a very low capacity, was gradually advanced by that diſcerning prince, on account of his abilities

ties and merit, until he attained the poſt of *treaſurer*, on the laſt expedition to Hindoſtan.

Ahmed Khan, taking advantage of the univerſal confuſion which ſucceeded the murder of the tyrant, found means to carry off a great part of his wealth, with the care of which he was entruſted by the nature of his employment, into ſome ſtrong receſſes in the hills near Ghôrebund in Zabûliſtan, which had been the reſidence of his anceſtors.—Here he was joined by ſuch of his tribe as had ſerved in Nadir Shah's army, and having collected together a body of thirty thouſand *Durânnees* (as the Afgans of this region are commonly called) iſſued forth into the neighbouring country, which being at preſent without any acknowledged head, was eaſily ſubjected to his authority; inſomuch that, in the courſe of two or three years, he laid the foundation of a new and powerful monarchy, aſſuming the title of *Ahmed-Shah Abdâllee*.

Ahmed Abdâllee, having perfectly established himself in his new acquisitions, began to turn his thoughts towards Hindostan, where the increasing imbecility of the empire gave him hopes of a success similar to that which had attended the expedition of his late master: and with this view he marched eastward, crossed the *Attuck*, and advanced through the country of *Punjab*, a short time before Allee Mahummed was appointed to Sirhind, as already related.—As Ahmed's army consisted of not less than sixty thousand well-appointed cavalry, when his intentions became known, the Sultan and his Amras, as well as all the inhabitants of Delhi and the surrounding country, who even yet severely felt the cruelties of Nadir Shah, were overwhelmed with terror and dejection.---The same intrigues however, which, on the incursion of Nadir Shah, had been so destructive to the public cause, did not at present exist; and the Vizier found himself at liberty to employ his integrity and vigour, unimpeded by the counter-plots which had then obſtructed their operation.

Meer Munnoo (the Vizier's ſon) was ordered to advance towards Lahore*, with ſuch forces as were then at Delhi, to watch Ahmed Shah's motions and retard his progreſs: — the farther preparations for defence were likely to have received a conſiderable check from the inſurrection of the Afgans in favour of Allee Mahummed; but that buſineſs being ſettled, and accounts daily arriving of the nearer approach of the Abdallee, the Vizier collected what remaining troops he could muſter from Rohilcund and other parts; and being farther reinforced by a conſiderable body of horſe under Sefdar Jung, proceeded to join his ſon, and oppoſe the invader.

The Vizier advanced to Sirhind, where he found Meer-Munnoo, who had not thought it prudent to venture farther on account of the great ſuperiority of

* p. 68.

the *Durânnees*; the united troops, having lodged all their heavy artillery and superfluous baggage in this place, purſued their route, and had proceeded three days march from thence, when they came within ſight of the enemy at a place called *Minôwrá*.——Here the adverſe armies, as if unwilling to bring matters to any ſudden deciſion, ſtrongly intrenched themſelves, and began their operations againſt each other by a diſtant cannonade, which was continued for many days, at intervals, without any material loſs on either ſide.---At length, it unfortunately happened that the Vizier was killed one evening by a random ſhot, in his tent:---His body was wrapped up in ſhawls by the attendants, and it was determined, in a council of the chief commanders, which was immediately convened upon this unhappy accident, to keep his death a profound ſecret, and to attack the enemy the very next morning, before a knowledge of this event ſhould have diſheartened the ſoldiers, who were known to place their chief dependance on the

the approved valour and abilities of the Vizier. Accordingly, a general action enſued next day, in which, after various ſucceſs, the troops of Ahmed Abdallee were at length repulſed, with the loſs of a conſiderable part of their artillery, and driven ſeveral miles from the field of battle. Ahmed, a few days after, once more tried his fortune againſt the Mogul forces, and was again defeated; but this able ſoldier, far from being diſmayed by theſe failures, at the very point when his fortune ſeemed to be moſt deſperate, ſuddenly turned the rear of the imperial army, and with a choſen body of cavalry puſhing to the eaſtward, nothing was heard of him for two days, and it was univerſally imagined that he had gone off towards Candahâr, when he ſeemed to ſpring up out of the earth before Sirhind, which immediately ſurrendered to him. Having levied a haſty contribution in that place, and plundered the neighbouring country, he retired as rapidly as he had advanced, and paſſing within four miles of the Mogul army in the night, proceeded towards the Punjab, carrying with him Fyzoola Khan and Abdoola Khan, the two ſons of Allee Mahummed whom the Rohilla had left as hoſtages of his fidelity, on his appointment to Sirhind,—as before mentioned. Theſe young men had accompanied the Vizier thus far, on his march to oppoſe Ahmed Abdallee; and had been ordered to remain at Sirhind, by which means they fell into the invader's hands, who conſidered them as the moſt valuable part of his acquiſition in this deſultory incurſion; as, by his power over them, he would be able to ſecure the neutrality of Allee Mahummed (whoſe abilities and enterpriſing diſpoſition he was well acquainted with)—and even to render him ſubſervient to his future views upon Hindoſtan.

The command of the Mogul army, which ſtill remained to the weſtward as a check upon Ahmed Abdallee, devolved upon the gallant Meer Munnoo, ſon of

the

the deceaſed Vizier, who had ſignally diſtinguiſhed himſelf in the late actions.

The old Sultan, Mahummed Shah, never recovered the ſhock which he ſuſtained in the death of his favourite, the faithful Kummir-ad-deen;—he died ſhortly after, and was ſucceeded in the imperial dignity by his ſon Ahmed, who appointed Sefdar Jung, the Subadar of Owde, to the high office of the *Vizaret.*

Conſidering all circumſtances, the repulſe of the Abdallee was certainly an event which could ſcarcely have been expected,—and ſerved, for the moment, to keep alive the dying embers of the royal power.—But, whilſt ſome remains of the empire were thus preſerved in one quarter, many of its provinces were alienated in another.

It has already been obſerved that Allee Mahummed ſtill entertained hopes of being able, ſome time or other, to recover the

Jagheers and other tenures which he had poſſeſſed in Rohilcund.

On his arrival at Sirhind, he immediately began to call together his ſcattered *banditti*, whom he gratified with whatever he could glean from the country which had in ſo weak a manner been entruſted to his charge; and in conſequence of his laviſh profuſeneſs to his followers, could make no remittances of revenue to Delhi;—he was, however, deterred from undertaking any thing openly, for the preſent, by the circumſtance of Meer Munnoo being for ſome time encamped near Sirhind with the advanced diviſion of the royal forces. When he heard that the Vizier was about to march from Delhi with the remainder of the Mogul army, in order to form a junction with Munnoo, he withdrew to Gungapore, a town about ſixteen miles diſtant from Sirhind, under pretence of collecting the rents of that Purgunna, but in reality to avoid an interview with the miniſter, and to evade any demands which might

might be made of him in the present exigency :---and, as soon as he understood that the Vizier had passed Sirhind, he proceeded immediately to the Ganges, and crossing that river at Biceghaut, marched directly into the heart of Rohilcund; and being there joined by the greatest part of his old retainers, presently possessed himself of all the countries which had formerly been in his hands, as well as the Jagheers of Kummir-ad-deen, Sefdar Jung, and others, comprehending almost the whole of Kuttâher.

As a great part of the royal forces had been withdrawn from these provinces to reinforce the main army under the Vizier, the few who were left never attempted any opposition to Allee Mahummed.—Some of the commanders he bought over to his interest; others he drove away; and the circumstances of the time preventing the possibility of any measures being taken to remedy his defection, he was left at full liberty to pursue every step which might be be neceſſary for his eſtabliſhment. He, by contributions and other means, raiſed conſiderable ſums, which he employed in levying troops, providing artillery-ſtores, building ſome forts and repairing others; and made ſo rapid a progreſs in his ſchemes, that when the government at Delhi was reſtored to tranquillity, he found himſelf able to make his own terms with the new Vizier; and in conſequence of a private bargain with the miniſter, obtained from the Emperor, ſoon after his acceſſion, grants of all thoſe territories he had lately ſeized, including the Jagheer of Moradabad, belonging to Kummir-ad-deen, but which had been vacated by his death, that of the Nizam conſiſting of the diſtrict of Barelli, that of Sefdar Jung conſiſting of Dampoor and Sheerkootch, together with other eſtates of many principal Amras; ſo that in fact, (if the grants of an impotent prince could be ſaid to beſtow any additional title) Allee Mahummed procured, as a ſubject of the Mogul government, a full and legal

authority

authority over the whole of Kuttaher*.

Nothing can afford ſo ſtrong an inſtance of the deplorable imbecility to which the court of Delhi was at this period reduced, and of the corruption or infatuation which reigned in its councils, than this conduct towards a man whoſe whole life had exhibited a continual ſeries of reſiſtance, and contempt of the imperial authority.—We have juſt ſeen an effort made to repel a formidable *foreign* foe, attended with ſucceſs; whilſt, from a want of interior political ſtamina, every Zimeendar raiſed the ſtandard of rebellion with ſucceſs, every lawleſs ruffian committed his enormities without fear of puniſhment, and every ſpecies of rapine and devaſtation were perpetrated without reſtraint!—but to return.

Allee Mahummed finding himſelf at length permanently fixed in what had ſo long been the object of his wiſhes, began immediately to ſettle the interior police of

* A. H. 1157---A. D. 1746.

the territory under proper regulations; and, that he might not be incommoded by the incurſions of the petty Rajahs, who held tracts along the foot of the Cummow hills, he rooted out all thoſe from whom he had any apprehenſions, and drove them to the other ſide of the Ganges, without any regard to their prior right in thoſe lands, which had been the ſeats of their anceſtors for many centuries. This was a mode of acting diametrically oppoſite to what had ever been obſerved by the Mahommedan ſettlers in Hindoſtan; the Rohilla chief, however, did not ſtop here; but conducted himſelf towards all the Hindoos of any rank or conſequence in Rohilcund (the only name by which Kuttaher was after this diſtinguiſhed) with a cruel and unjuſtifiable ſeverity. He deprived ſuch as were Zimeendars of their lands, and the public officers of their employments, and filled the places thus vacated with his creatures; ſo that in the ſpace of a few months the country was put completely under a Patan government. This decided

decided mode of proceeding, although harſh and tyrannical, yet was certainly the only means of ſecuring Allee Mahummed in that abſolute independence at which he aimed, as it formed a combination apparently too ſtrong to be ſhaken or deranged by any meaſures the court of Delhi might in future adopt for the recovery of its dominion, leaving the revenue of every diſtrict at his ſole diſpoſal, and opening to him the moſt ſecret ſources of intelligence;---and accordingly we do not find that, during the remainder of his life, any attempt was made to diſturb or ſubvert the deſpotic authority of the Afgans in Rohilcund.

Had the life of Allee Mahummed been prolonged, it is certain that he would have raiſed this country to a high degree of happineſs and proſperity; as, being altogether unmoleſted by other interference, he employed his whole time in making various wiſe and ſalutary regulations, placing his army on a reſpectable footing, and correcting and arranging the different departments

ments of government with a ſkill which diſtinguiſhed his character as much for his policy and prudence in the exerciſe of power, as his preceding actions, for the perſeverance and enterprize by which that power was acquired.

But the time ſoon arrived, when Allee Mahummed, in common with other ſucceſsful heroes, was to prove and experience the idle vanity of all the purſuits of ambition.

He had for ſome years been ſubject to periodical returns of deafneſs, but without any material injury to his health in other reſpects;—this diſorder, about fourteen months after his reinſtatement in Rohilcund, returned upon him with uncommon violence, inſomuch that it is ſaid he could not hear the report of a cannon; he was at the ſame time ſeized with a dropſy which baffled the ſkill of the phyſicians; and finding that this laſt diſeaſe increaſed upon him, and that his diſſolution approached, he he was anxious to put affairs on ſuch a footing as would ſecure the inheritance of his territories to his children.

As all his ſons were ſtill under age, Allee Mahummed was ſufficiently aware that the transfer of the government into any *one* hand until their maturity would be likely to defeat his intention;—but he hoped by a judicious partition of the whole power among a number of the principal individuals for that period, to create a counterpoiſe of intereſts in the community, which might eventually operate in favour of his heirs.

He therefore called together all the chief perſons of the Rohilla party; and it is on this occaſion that the firſt mention is made of Rahmut Khan and Doondy Khan, as bearing any part in the tranſactions in Rohilcund: the former of theſe was the uncle and the latter the couſin of Allee Mahummed:—they had heretofore moved in a very humble ſphere; but their

* See Page 5.

relation, upon his final eſtabliſhment in that quarter, had beſtowed upon them the charge of ſome of his moſt important diſtricts in the territories of Baréllee, and Biſſoolee. He now conſtituted the former of theſe *Hafiz*, or chief *Guardian* of his children during their minority; he likewiſe joined Doondy Khan in the guardianſhip appointing him commandant of the troops. He in their preſence executed a will, in which he directed that, until the return of his two eldeſt ſons, Fyzoola Khan and Abdoola Khan, (who had been carried off by Ahmed Abdâllee to Candahâr) the ſupreme government ſhould, under the direction and control of the guardians, be veſted in his third ſon, Sydoola Khan; and he received from the guardians the moſt ſolemn promiſes and aſſurances of their inviolable attachment to all his children, which they ratified by oath upon the Koran. Theſe men were, of courſe, to be neceſſarily entruſted with a principal ſhare in the executive authority;—but as a check on the dangerous influence

fluence with which they would hereby become vested, he united with them his kinsmen, Niâmut Khan and Sillabut Khan, in the general administration of affairs. He also created two principal officers of state; —Futté Khan, one of his most favourite retainers, who had invariably adhered to his interests in every change of his fortune, he nominated to the post of *Khansaman*, or steward; and Serdar Khan to that of *Buxy*, or paymaster, to act immediately under the regents. To all these Allee Mahummed gave the government of different districts, which they respectively swore to hold in trust for his children. The whole were, upon every emergency, to consult together for the good of the general state; and, in case of necessity, each was to lead his proportion of forces into the field, and to pay a *quota* into the grand treasury under the Buxy for the disbursement of contingencies. Allee Mahummed's last care, previous to his decease, was to discharge, with a scrupulous exactness, all the arrears due to his troops; he also diſtributed an *advance* among them to the amount of twenty-five lacks of rupees, taking an acknowledgement from every individual, by which each ſolemnly bound himſelf to ſtand by and adhere to the cauſe of his family; and theſe acknowledgements were lodged in the *Toſhek-Khané*, or chancery, under the care of Fûtté Khan, khanſaman.

Allee Mahummed did not long ſurvive the new arrangement of the Rohilla government; and the circumſtances of his death were not leſs remarkable than the whole tenor of his life. On the morning of his deceaſe, he was carried into the Durbar, where were aſſembled all the principal perſons with whom he entruſted the management of his territories.—Here he publicly declared the particulars of his will, in which he had ſettled the different diviſions of the country upon his ſons, according to a diſtribution therein mentioned;—and intreating their protection of his children, he expired

expired amidſt the united murmurs of ſorrow and applauſe, on the 4th of the ſecond *Jemmâd*, in the 1160th year of the Higera*, after acquiring a great and laſting reputation among his countrymen.

Allee Mahummed, at his death, left ſix ſons, whoſs names have been already mentioned†; the two eldeſt of theſe were ſtill with Ahmed Abdallee at Candahar ‡; the remaining four,—to wit, Sydoola Khan, Mahummed-Yâr Khan, Allah-Yâr Khan, and Murtooza Khan, being yet infants, were committed for the preſent to the charge of Futté Khan, khanſaman, and the guardians provided an adequate eſtabliſhment for their ſupport.

The death of Allee Mahummed opened the way for ſeveral attempts to overſet the Afgan intereſts in Rohilcund, and to drive them from their uſurped poſſeſſions.

---

* A.D. 1749. † Page 70. ‡ Page 80.

With this intention, Kûttub-ad-deen, the grandſon of Azmut Oolah, repaired to Delhi, and with eaſe obtained a *Firman* for the ſucceſſion to the Fowjdarrey of Moradabad. But the power of the court was now reduced ſo low, that it could not afford any aſſiſtance to its ſervants to enforce the royal mandates: orders were every day iſſued which never were obeyed, and diſtricts granted which could never be ſubdued.—Kûttub-ad-deen fatally experienced the truth of this obſervation:—marching into Rohilcund under the ſanction of the royal commiſſion, but with a force by no means equal to ſuch an undertaking, he was met at Dampoor by the Rohilla troops under Doondy Khan, who entirely defeated him, and put all his followers to the ſword.

Scarcely was this diſturbance quelled, before another more formidable enemy appeared to contend with.

Some years previous to the events we have been

been relating, the Afgans of the Bungiſh tribe had made a ſettlement at Ferrochabad, which from the ſubſequent imbecility and increaſing weakneſs of the court, had ſince been (like many other parts of the empire) erected into a ſort of independent principality; paying only a nominal tribute, and acknowledging the authority of the Mogul government, but without exhibiting any real proofs of dependance upon it.—Kâeem Jung Bungiſh was, at the period here treated of, chief of that tribe, and was ſtiled "*Nabob of Ferrochabad.*"—He entertained the ſame hopes which had deluded Kûttub-ad-deen, of profiting by the death of Allee Mahummed, concluding that the Afgan chiefs in Rohilcund, being deprived of their uſual firm ſupport by this event, would eaſily yield to the firſt impreſſion he ſhould attempt to make in that quarter. He accordingly prepared a numerous army, and a formidable train of artillery; and croſſing the Ganges on a bridge of boats at Futty-Ghur, proceeded up the erſtern bank of that river, on pretence of ſeeking ſatisfaction for ſome encroachments which had been made upon him by the Rohillas, and ſome affronts his people had received from them in the ſmall portion of his territory which lay on that ſide of the river.

The chiefs in Rohilcund, when they were certified of Kâeem Jung's intention, were at firſt ſtruck with terror and diſmay; as they were well acquainted with his power and bravery, and their government had not yet attained a ſufficient degree of firmneſs to enable it to withſtand ſuch a ſhock without manifeſt danger. The two eldeſt ſons of Allee Mahummed were moreover abſent; and the third, in whom the oſtenſible authority of the ſtate was veſted, was as yet a child, whoſe preſence could inſpire but little ſtability in their councils, or valour in the field. The guardians therefore ſent ambaſſadors to Kâeem Jung, in the moſt ſuppliant terms, to deprecate his reſentment, and offering to ſurrender to him the whole territory they were poſ-

ſeſſed

ſeſſed of to the weſtward of the Ganges ;—they likewiſe repreſented to him the ill policy of the Afgan powers quarrelling with and diſabling each other, at a time when their force ſhould rather be combined to reſiſt the machinations of their common enemies.

All this reaſoning, however, had no effect upon Kâeem Jung, who was determined to aim at nothing leſs than the total ſubjugation of Rohilcund ; and the ſumiſſive profeſſions of the chiefs indicating a great degree of confuſion and alarm, induced him the more obſtinately to perſiſt. The Rohillas were therefore obliged to provide againſt the worſt.

The guardians and other miniſters aſſembled their forces, and ſet young Sydoola Khan at their head, in hopes that his preſence, by reminding the ſoldiers of their former ſucceſs under his father, might be regarded by them as a propitious circumſtance, and be attended with ſome good effect.

Kâeem Jung advanced to Owde, and from thence attempted, by directing his route to the eaſtward, to penetrate into the heart of Rohilcund.

Shortly after, the adverſe armies met upon the plains of Dowrey, about fourteen miles from Owlah, where a bloody engagement enſued, in which, after a variety of ſucceſs, Kâeem Jung being ſlain by a matchlock ſhot, his troops at length gave way, and were totally routed.

The Rohillas after this victory ſeized on all the poſſeſſions of Kâeem Jung, to the eaſtward of the Ganges.

Sefdar Jung, who had by this time acquired an unbounded authority at Delhi, reigning over the Emperor himſelf as well as the *Amras* of the court with an abſolute ſway, was much pleaſed at this breach between

tween the Afgan powers, whoſe growing influence in the northern provinces was greatly dreaded by him; and had indeed been no inconſiderable check upon his ambitious deſigns;—nor was the conſequent defeat and death of Kâeem Jung leſs agreeable to him, as that chief had often treated the orders of the ſupreme government, and the Emperor's requiſitions of ſupplies for the ſervice of the ſtate, with the moſt contemptuous indifference and neglect; and theſe events afforded an opportunity for recovering the dominion of Ferrochabad, and ſeizing on the treaſure and effects of the deceaſed as a puniſhment for his contumacy. With this deſign the Vizier marched from Delhi at the head of a conſiderable force, and inveſted Ferrochabad.

Kâeem Jung's family having been left at Ferrochabad without any protection, were in no condition to oppoſe Sefdar Jung, and endeavoured to make their peace, by ſurrendering to him their whole property;—but he, in order to prevent any future attempt tempts to revenge this extortion in behalf of the Emperor, ſeized Kâeem Jung's mother, and ſome others of his relations, and ſent them to the fort of Allehabad; —determining to hold them as hoſtages for the future demeanour of their party.

In the mean time, Ahmed Khan Bungiſh, the brother of Kâeem Jung, after the battle of Dowrey, collected the remains of the defeated troops at Maw. Here he was joined by his brother's wife, who had contrived to effect her eſcape from Ferrochabad, and brought with her ſome money and jewels, and a few faithful followers. Theſe propitious events ſerved to ſupport the declining ſpirit of the Ferrochabad Afgans; and numbers of them flocked in every day from all parts of the country to the ſtandard of Ahmed. This ſoon enabled him to proceed to action; and he preſently marched to Ferrochabad, drove the troops of Sefdar Jung out of that city, and put to death all thoſe who had been any

way

way inſtrumental in the misfortunes of his family.

Rajah Newel Rây, who was a favourite retainer of Sefdar, and acted as his deputy in the province of Oude, immediately marched with a great army from that place to attempt the recovery of Ferrochabad.

Ahmed Khan Bungiſh had by this time ſo much ſtrengthened himſelf, that he took the reſolution of marching out to meet the deputy, who had paſſed over the Ganges at Kinnoge, about thirty miles below Ferrochabad, and was already ſome way advanced on his route towards that city. Their forces engaged upon the banks of the Calli-Nudee (a ſmall river which runs into the Ganges) and after an obſtinate conflict, the Rajah being at length ſlain, his troops fled on every quarter.—Ahmed Khan purſued them for ſeveral coſs from the field of battle with terrible ſlaughter; and following his blow, he croſſed the Ganges on the bridge of boats which Newel Rây had conſtructed

conſtructed upon that river at Kinnoge, and marching directly to Oude, ſeized on all the treaſure and effects of Sefdar Jung.

The Vizier, incenſed at this overthrow, moſt baſely and cruelly cauſed all the individuals of the Bungiſh family, whom he had impriſoned, to be put death; and taking forty pieces of the royal artillery from Delhi, marched in perſon with what force he could muſter againſt Ahmed, who immediately returned from Oude toward the Ganges, and paſſing over on the bridge of boats before mentioned, diſpoſed a part of his troops ſo as effectually to cover the territory of Ferrochabad, and with the remainder prepared directly to meet and engage the royal forces. This boldneſs intimidating the cowardly Vizier; and after ſome ſkirmiſhes, in which Ahmed Khan was generally ſucceſsful, the contending parties at length met on a large plain near the village of *Pattiáree*, within twelve miles of Ferrochabad, where enſued one of the fierceſt engagements recorded in the ſtruggles

ſtruggles of the declining empire.——At firſt, the action, from the ſuperiority of forces (particularly artillery) ſeemed rather to incline in favour of the royal army; but during the hotteſt part of the engagement there ſuddenly aroſe a *ſand-ſtorm*, (common in thoſe parts of India) which blew with violence directly in the faces of the Moguls; and the Afgans, improving this advantage, ruſhed on in the boſom of a thick cloud of duſt, and charged their enemies with irreſiſtible impetuoſity.—The Vizier's troops being blinded by the ſand, could neither judge of the number, nor diſtinguiſh the attack of their aſſailants; their panick was increaſed by the whirlwind and darkneſs which ſurrounded them, and in a few minutes they gave way and fled with the utmoſt precipitation. All the Vizier's artillery was taken, and his infantry cut off to a man.—He himſelf eſcaped with difficulty, and two days after arrived at Delhi in a tranſport of rage and deſpair. He now reſolved, at all events, utterly to extirpate the Afgans, and to risk the existence of his own power, and of the ruinous remains of the empire, to effect his purpose, by calling in the aid of the Hindoo powers, whose alliance was scarcely less destructive than their enmity.

In pursuance of this resolution, he drew the whole of the money out of the royal treasury; and finding this to be insufficient, laid Delhi and the neighbouring country under a heavy contribution.—He next entered into a treaty with the Mahratta chiefs, Apa-Jee and Mulhar-Row, procuring their alliance by giving them a large sum in advance, and bonds to a considerable amount, in consequence of which they joined him with a body of fifty thousand horse.—By similar means he procured the assistance of Soorâj Mull with a number of Jâts.

With these united forces the Vizier advanced once more towards Ferrochabad.

Ahmed Khan prepared to oppose them; but

but finding himſelf unable to contend, alone, with ſo powerful a confederacy, he applied to the Rohilla chiefs for aſſiſtance, repreſenting this as a common cauſe, in which the whole of the Afgan powers ſhould feel themſelves equally concerned. Theſe chiefs, however, were much averſe to involving themſelves in a quarrel, from the moſt favourable iſſue of which they could derive no eſſential benefit, and in caſe of defeat had every think to fear;—they would not, therefore, pay any attention to this repreſentation; upon which Ahmed Khan ſent his mother, who was a woman of great art, and poſſeſſed of a maſculine underſtanding, to endeavour to negotiate an alliance with the Rohillas, and to ſettle all matters of diſpute that had ariſen between them and Kâeem Jung.

The Begum accordingly repaired to Kuttaher, and applied ſeverally to the chiefs, but to no purpoſe; they declared "that "they had no objection to compromiſe "every diſpute with the Bungiſh family; "but,

" but, that they could by no means think " of involving themſelves in a new quar- " rel with the united forces of the Empe- " ror, the Jâts, and the Mahrattas, the " event of which muſt, in ſome reſpects, " be prejudicial to them, and might prove " totally runious to their intereſts."—— As a laſt reſource, the old Begum waited on Sydoola Khan, and uſing every artful inſinuation that could flatter his vanity or inflame his ambition, at length perſuaded him to take a part in Ahmed's quarrel with the Vizier, notwithſtanding the ſtrong remonſtrances of the guardians and other ancient chiefs :—he accordingly prepared to join Ahmed, accompanied only by Futtee Khan and his troops, as Hafiz Rahmut and Doondee Khan ſo entirely diſapproved of this raſh proceeding, that they poſitively refuſed to take any part in it.

The Rohillas do not appear, on this occaſion, to have acted with much ſyſtematick prudence.—By permitting a *part* of their forces to join Ahmed Khan they drew

upon

upon themſelves the reſentment of a power which, if ſucceſsful in the firſt inſtance, they would not be able to withſtand;—or, by ſuffering a narrow and ſelfiſh policy to outweigh every more remote conſideration, they, in the wilful ſacrifice of a natural ally, laid the foundation of their own misfortunes.

Whilſt theſe tranſactions took place in Rohilcund, Ahmed Khan, in the mean time, finding himſelf utterly unable to attempt any oppoſition againſt the prodigious force of the Vizier, evacuated Ferrochabad, and croſſing the Ganges at Futty Ghur, deſtroyed the boats upon that river for many miles, and joined Sydoola Khan at Amraopore.—The whole Afgan force, when united, did not much exceed fifteen thouſand men.

Sefdar Jung, when he arrived at Ferrochabad, finding that place deſolate, immediately diſpatched a body of Mahratta horſe to ſeize the boats at Ramgâut, about ſeventy miles higher up the river.

It would appear that the allied army of the Afgans was not properly diſpoſed, or that the commanders were not ſufficiently active in defending the paſſages of the river, which Sefdar Jung, in a few days, croſſed at the above place, with little oppoſition. This neceſſarily obliged the Afgans, who had before advanced to the ſouthward, to fall haſtily back in order to cover Rohilcund. Sefdar Jung halted for ſome days at Aſſidpore, near the fords, and from thence wrote to Sydoola Khan and Futtee Khan, requiring them immediately to forſake the Bungiſh chief, and repair to the royal ſtandard.—He alſo diſpatched *Firmans* in the name of the Emperor, to the other Rohilla chiefs, demanding the Mogul government's proportion of the revenues for the laſt three years, which they had never rendered any account of.

The guardians now felt the fatal effects

of

of that equivocal and indecifive mode of conduct which they had adopted, in fuffering one of their body to engage in this difpute. They found themfelves involved, and they muft either take an active part, and openly rebel againft the acknowledged authority of their fovereign, or fubmit to fuch terms as might be impofed upon them. It may readily be conceived that they adopted the former alternative :—inftead, therefore, of returning any direct anfwer to the aforefaid demand, they propofed to join the other confederate Afgans with their forces, in order to oppofe the Vizier ;—but before this junction could be effected, Sefdar Jung, aware of their intentions, marched directly to attack Ahmed Khan and his allies, who fell back at his approach, wifhing to avoid an action until they fhould be reinforced ; but the imperial forces ftill continuing to prefs upon them, a battle enfued in the neighbourhood of Iflamnagurr, fourteen miles from Biffoolee, in which the Afgans, from the irresistable superiority of the enemy, were soon totally routed and dispersed.

An universal panick immediately spread among all the Afgans throughout the Rohilla territories.—The guardians carried off Allee Mahummed's children to Owlah, and finding no safety there, fled with their families and treasure to a strong post in the Cummôw hills, a short distance above Lolldông.—Here they intrenched themselves, and rendered their situation impregnable against any sudden attack; which they were allowed abundant leisure to accomplish by the uaccountable dilatoriness of their enemies, who, instead of prosecuting their blow with vigour, halted near the field of battle several days, and afterwards advanced towards the hills by very easy marches.——At length, when the imperial troops arrived before the post which the Rohillas occupied, Sefdar Jung, judgeing it extremely hazardous to attempt an attack, resolved to form a sort of blockade, in hopes of reducing them by famine; and when his heavy artillery arrived (which had been delayed in their approach by the thickneſs of the woods and the badneſs of the roads) he commenced a cannonade againſt the Rohilla works, but with little effect. The Afgans, during theſe operations, made many ſallies, and ſome with conſiderable ſucceſs: they alſo found means to be ſupplied with proviſions from the hills in their rear ſufficient to ſubſiſt them for ſome months;--but they became ſickly from the unhealthfulneſs of the place in which they were pent up, and muſt ſoon have been reduced, had not the intrigues of the court, and the obſtructions Sefdar Jung met with in his own army, contributed to their deliverance.

Whilſt the Vizier was proſecuting his operations againſt the Rohillas, advices were received from Delhi that Ahmed Abdallee, having repulſed the royal forces, was marching againſt that place with a large army; determined, as was ſuppoſed, to depoſe Ahmed Shah, and eſtabliſh himſelf upon the imperial throne. The Emperor, at the ſame time, wrote to the Vizier with his own hand, requiring him in the moſt preſſing terms to return directly to court; and he moreover found himſelf greatly embarraſſed by the clamours of his allies, the Jâts and Mahrattas, who were already weary of the tedious ſervice in which he had engaged them, and which was ſo ill ſuited to their ideas and habits of warfare; —a ſevere ſickneſs, alſo, began to rage in his camp. In the perplexity occaſioned by all theſe untoward circumſtances, Sefdar Jung found himſelf, unwillingly, conſtrained to accede to the offer propoſed to him by the Rohillas; and he agreed to grant them a peace, on the ſlender foundation of their delivering him bonds to the amount of fifty lacks of rupees, to be diſcharged out of the enſuing collections of the country; with a promiſe of paying every year in future, a *peiſhkuſh*, or quit-rent, of five lacks to the Emperor, of whom they ſolemnly profeſſed to hold their territories in fealty. The bonds, the obligations of which the Rohillas

Rohillas had not the moſt diſtant idea of ever fulfilling, were delivered by Sefdar Jung to the Mahratta commander, Mulhar Row, as a ſecurity for a part of the ſubſidy ſtill remaining due to him*; and, on the before-mentioned terms, the Afgans were reinſtated in all their former poſſeſſions, and affairs in Rohilcund once more bore the appearance of tranquillity†.

The circumſtance which had ſo ſuddenly recalled the Vizier to Delhi, proved to be only a falſe alarm.

Ahmed Abdâllee had paſſed the *Jenâub*‡, and laid the country to the eaſt-

* It may not here be improper to remark that this event, however remotely, may be conſidered as the *origin* of all the ſubſequent revolutions in Rohilcund; being the foundation of the Mahratta claims in that quarter.

† A. H. 1164.—A. C. 1753.

‡ One of the five rivers which, watering the territory of Punjab, fall into the *Indus* in the province of *Moultan*.

ward of that river under contribution;—but it does not appear that he had any farther intentions at that time; as, on the approach of a part of the Mogul army under Meer Munnoo, he again retreated towards Candahâr, without offering to come to action. This desultory expedition, however, afforded an opportunity to some of the Afgan Amras at court, who favoured the cause of the Rohillas, and hated the Vizier, to impede the operations of the latter, by greatly exaggerating the danger of the empire from the incursions of the Abdâllees; and the Emperor, as we have seen, weakly entered into the views of these nobles, in pressing him to return. Thus was lost the only opportunity that perhaps should ever occur, of totally subverting the power of the rebellious Afgans, and reducing these provinces to complete subjection.

It was on this incursion that Ahmed Abdâllee, in order to attach the Rohillas to his interest, released Abdoola Khan and Fyzoola

Fyzoola Khan, the ſons of Allee Mahummed, and loading them with preſents, permitted them to depart for Lahore, where they were met by ſome Rohilla commanders, who conducted them to *Kuttâher*.—— The Abdâllee, at the ſame time, wrote letters to Hafiz Rahmut and the other chiefs, ſtrongly recommending a ſtrict attention to the will of Allee Mahummed, and requiring them to receive and acknowledge theſe young men and their brothers as his proper heirs, and to eſtabliſh them forthwith in their inheritance.

On the approach of the brothers, they were met at Banghaut upon the Ganges, by the guardians, who received them with every poſſible mark of diſtinction and reſpect, and accompanied them to Oulah, where their four younger brothers at this period reſided.

Here the ſons of Allee Mahummed lived together a ſhort time with great cordiality and ſatisfaction; but ſome trifling diſputes

disputes arising from so many of them residing in the same place, where each was attended by a numerous train of dependants, whose frequent squabbles gave occasion for continual altercation, it was judged expedient by the guardians to separate them; and, in a general council of the chiefs held upon the occasion, it was determined to effect this by investing them with their inheritance.

Even in this first execution of their trust, however, the guardians deviated considerably from the will of Allee Mahummed:—instead of putting his sons into possession of the respective portions of inheritance therein specified, an equal partition was made of all his acquisitions and usurpations into three parts, each valued at thirteen lacks annual produce, which were allotted to the three eldest brothers respectively; and the three youngest were severally provided for as coheirs with the others.

By this arrangement, Abdoola Khan and

and Murtooza Khan got Owlah, and the countries to the northward; Fyzoola Khan and Mahummed Yar, Barellee; and Sydoola Khan and Allah-Yar Khan, Moradabad;—and a treaty of perpetual friendſhip and alliance being executed by the brothers, Sydoola Khan proceeded to take poſſeſſion of his government at Moradabad, and Abdoola Khan and Fyzoola Khan remained at Owlah.

But, however anxious the guardians might appear to eſtabliſh and ſecure the intereſts of their wards by the above partition, it is certain they by no means deſigned that it ſhould be a *laſting* one. If the brothers continued upon terms of mutual amity and good underſtanding with each other, as they muſt ſoon arrive at maturity, the conſequence and power of the guardians and other miniſters throughout the country would ceaſe of courſe. Under this apprehenſion, and actuated by an ambition which overlooks every obſtacle, and overleaps every bound of honour and virtue,

they

they determined to adopt ſuch meaſures as muſt effectually overſet the intentions of Allee Mahummed, and leave the management of the government at all times entirely in their own power.—To obtain this end, nothing appeared ſo well calculated as ſowing the ſeeds of diſſenſion and diſtruſt among the family of Allee Madummed: as ſoon, therefore, as Fyzoola Khan and his brother were ſettled at Owlah, the creatures and emiſſaries placed about them by the guardians begun, by the moſt artful inſinuations, to excite a diſagreement and jealouſy between them, reſpecting the claims of ſome of their followers: this, at firſt, occaſioned only ſome ſmall bickerings, but theſe ſoon broke out into an open quarrel.

A riot enſued, one morning, among their domeſticks; it had originated in ſome very trifling circumſtances: but each of the brothers warmly eſpouſing the cauſe of his own ſervants, and the minds of all

being

being already ſufficiently inflamed by the underhand practices of thoſe employed for that purpoſe, the diſturbance ſoon became general. Both parties flew to arms,—and every thing bore the appearance of the moſt alarming inſurrection. In the midſt of this confuſion, a number of Rohillas found an opportunity to gratify their cuſtomary avidity for pillage, by plundering the *bazars* of Owlah.—At length, night, and the interference of Hafiz Rahmut and Doondee Khan, helped to quell the uproar.

The guardians had now a ſpecious pretext for carrying the preface to their projected ſcheme into execution; and ſoon after, accuſing Abdoola Khan and his adherents of having been the firſt aggreſſors in the foregoing affray, they ſentenced him to be deprived of his ſhare in the government, and baniſhed him to the other ſide of the Ganges:——thither he was voluntarily accompanied by his brothers, Allah Yar and Mahummed Yar. This violent meaſure, however, excited ſuch univerſal diſguſt among the numerous retainers to Allee Mahummed's family, that the guardians ſoon found themſelves conſtrained to make ſome alteration in their plan; —therefore, after having previouſly ſuperſeded the ſeniority of Abdoola Khan by inveſting his brother Sydoola Khan with the oſtenſible inſignia of authority, they thought proper to recal the former, and ſettled upon him the diſtricts of Sehſwan, Oojânee and Shiddad-Naggûrr, producing between four and five lacks annual revenue, and to the ſecond of the above places he ſhortly after retired, determining altogether to ſeclude himſelf from any farther concern in publick affairs.——At the ſame time, under pretence of the youth and inexperience of Fyzoola Khan, the guardians took out of his hands the management of thoſe countries which had fallen to his lot in the general partition, and ſettled upon him a ſmall diſtrict of five lacks, including the Purgûnnas of Rampore, Shawbad and Chatcheet; and Fyzoola Khan ſoon after repaired to the city of Rampore, which place has from that period been his principal reſidence.

Having

Having thus removed the chief obſtacles to their views, the guardians proceeded, without farther reſerve, to the completion of them, and made the *real* partition of the Rohilla dominion among themſelves, which they had intended from the time of Allee Mahummed's death.

By this new ſettlement, Hafiz Rahmut got the diſtricts of Barêllee and Peeleabete; Morâdabad fell to the ſhare of Doondy Khan, together with the country extending from thence to the city of Biſſoolee; —and the diſtricts of Owlah, Budâvon, Owſte, Koot and Ahrat were equally divided between Sirdar Khan, the Buxy, and Futtee Khan, the Khanſaman; an acquiſition which was ſufficient to detach them from the intereſts of the heirs of their former maſter. As no territory was ſettled upon Sydoola Khan, whom the guardians, to ſerve their own purpoſes, ſtill continued to ſupport in the ſtation to which they had raiſed him, a proviſion was made for him by a penſion of eight lacks per annum, of which

which two were furniſhed by the Khanſaman, three by Hafiz Rahmut, and three by Doondee Khan. No attention whatever was paid to three younger ſons of Allee Mahummed in this adjuſtment, and they were left either to ſtarve, or reſpectively to depend upon their brothers, according to the firſt ſettlement.—" Thus" (to uſe the emphatick expreſſions of the Rohilla hiſtorian)—" giving their honour " to the winds, and ſuffering the tide of " avarice and ambition to ſweep away the " dying injunctions of their benefactor in- " to the ocean of oblivion, the guardians " iniquitouſly deprived the children of " Allee Mahummed of their birthright, " and ſeized the reins of authority with " the hand of ingratitude !"——But this revolution*, although it changed the property, did not make any material alteration in the ſtate with reſpect to its conſtitutional arrangement, and the publick buſineſs con-

* A. H. 1165---A. D. 1754.

tinued

tinued to be carried on in the ſame train as formerly.

Sydoola Khan, who was a young man of high ſpirit, being exceedingly incenſed at the iniquitous proceedings of Hafiz Rahmut, and his colleagues, retired from Owlah in diſguſt. Murtooza Khan, from the ſame motive, went off to Secundera-bâd, where he ſoon after died: and his brother, Allah Yâr, was about this time ſeized with a conſumption, which in a few weeks proved fatal to him.

We have here related all the principal domeſtick tranſactions of the Rohillas, until the ultimate ſettlement of their internal ſyſtem:—but they had not, in the mean time, remained idle ſpectators of the contending ſtruggles of the various newly-eſtabliſhed powers around them; and ſeveral incidents occurred, during the period we have been treating of, which, in their events greatly tended to the increaſe of their political weight and influence, as well as to the extenſion of their dominion.

Sefdar Jung, not very long after the fruitleſs event of his laſt expedition againſt the Rohillas, having murdered Juneid Khan, the favourite of the Emperor, Ahmed Shah, and committed many other enormities, was, by that monarch deprived of the *Vizaret*, and degraded from his rank; in conſequence of which he rebelled againſt his ſovereign, and even beſieged him in his capital: but he was fruſtrated in all his efforts, by the ſuperior bravery and abilities of Ghazee-ad-deen Khan, who commanded in Delhi under the Emperor; and being compelled to relinquiſh this undertaking, retired to Owde, where he ſhortly after died, and was ſucceeded in his dominion by his ſon, Suja-al-Dowlah, who, however, did not obtain any *royal deed*, by which he might oſtenſibly fix his claim to the ſucceſſion, until ſome time after. This prince, who, whatever defects of character he might labour under, was an an artful and able politician, foreseeing the approaching distresses of the empire, totally withdrew himself for a time from all connections with the court, and wisely gave his whole attention to the regulation of the interior œconomy of his government, and the provision of such means of defence as might secure him from the effect of any change which should happen to take place in the Mogul administration.

Soon after the decease of Sefdar Jung, Ghazee-ad-deen, who now possessed the whole power at court, having reason to apprehend that Ahmed Shah, who equally dreaded and hated him, had formed a plan for his destruction, deposed the unfortunate Emperor, and deprived him of his sight; and releasing from confinement the prince Yâaz-ad-deen, who (with many others of the royal family) had passed the greatest part of his life within the walls of a prison, set him upon the throne, under the title of "*Allumgeer the Second.*"

Suja-al-Dowlah had ever dreaded the abilities and growing power of Ghazee-ad-deen, whoſe principles he knew to be as flagitious as his ambition was unbounded. This laſt bold meaſure had left all the remaining force and riches of the empire at that miniſter's diſpoſal; and he had lately made ſome overtures to an alliance with Ahmed Khan Bungiſh (who on the capitulation of the Rohillas to Sefdar Jung hâd been ſuffered to return to Ferrochabad, and to re-eſtabliſh himſelf there) by flattering him with a promiſe of appointing him to the office of *Meer Buxy*, or paymaſter of the empire, evidently with a view to procure his aſſiſtance in a plan which Ghazee-ad-deen had at this time formed for the conqueſt of Oude, as a fief of the Mogul empire, the grant of which had ceaſed on the death of the former Subadâr.

Suja-al-Dowlah was not a little diſconcerted upon the diſcovery of the miniſter's deſigns; and as he was willing to embrace every poſſible means of ſtrengthening himſelf

ſelf againſt the approaching danger, he diſpatched ambaſſadors with conſiderable preſents to the Rohilla chiefs, and wrote a letter to young Sydoola Khan, (whoſe elder brothers had not, as yet, been liberated by Ahmed Adâllee) requeſting his friendſhip, and repreſenting how much the common intereſt of all independent ſtates was concerned in withſtanding the preſent intentions of the miniſter.

The chiefs, on the receipt of the Subadâr of Oude's letters, did not long deliberate on what part they ſhould act.—They well knew that, in the event of the ſubjugation of Suja-al-Dowlah, their own overthrow would be a certain conſequence; as they had already incurred the penalties of diſobedience and breach of faith by neglecting to fulfil any one of the articles of their late capitulation; and, in caſe of being attacked by Ghazee-ad-deen, had nothing to hope for from the factions at court, which had formerly impeded the operations of Sefdar Jung. They therefore returned a favourable anſwer, and, within a few weeks, entered into a formal treaty of alliance with Suja-al-Dowlah; each party mutually engaging to ſupport the other againſt all enemies.

Mean time, Ghazee-ad-deen having effected his treaty with Ahmed Khan Bungiſh, arrived at Ferrochabad with a conſiderable army; and was there joined by that chief with a body of twenty thouſand Patâns.—From hence he marched to Mindy-Ghaut, and conſtructing a bridge of boats upon the Ganges, advanced to Goojer-poor, on the eaſtern ſide of the river, and diſpatched a meſſage to Suja-al-Dowlah, demanding in the Emperor's name, the immediate ceſſion of the country; and requiring him forthwith to deliver up the treaſure and jewels of his deceaſed father, forfeited by his diſobedience and rebellion. To this peremptory meſſage the Nabob returned an evaſive anſwer, and opened a negociation with Ghazee-ad-deen, merely with a view to create delay: he had, in

the

the interim, repeatedly diſpatched expreſſes to the Rohillas, informing them of the imminent danger in which he ſtood.—— At length, the chiefs collecting the whole of their forces, proceeded to his relief.

As the Rohilla army amounted to upwards of thirty thouſand men, Ghazee-addeen judged it prudent to endeavour to draw them off from their connection with the Subadâr; and for this purpoſe he cauſed a *Firman*, under the royal ſeal, to be directed to Sydoola Khan, "requiring the aſſiſtance "of the Afgans againſt the rebellious ſon "of the traitor, Sefdar Jung."—The Rohillas, however, underſtood their own intereſt too well to join in the views of the miniſter, as they were fully aware of the depth of his policy and the boldneſs and extent of his deſigns, and knew that the inevitable conſequence of Suja-al Dowlah's defeat muſt be their own extirpation from their aſſumed dominion in Kuttâher. —They therefore adhered firmly to the cauſe of their ally, inſiſted on the royal

 forces

forces immediately evacuating his territories, and took post in such a situation that Ghazee-ad-deen could not have attempted to advance without risking an engagement; and apprehending that his army would by no means be an equal match for the united forces of his opponents, the minister agreed to compromise the business with Suja-al-Dowlah for the small sum of five lacks of rupees, and an obligation to pay to the Emperor an annual tribute to the same amount in future; and the cash being paid, and the proper bonds executed by the Nabob, and guaranteed by the counter-signature of Sydoola Khan in the name of the Rohilla states, the royal forces returned towards Delhi; and the Rohillas marched back to their own country.

It was about this period that Ahmed Abdâllee released the two eldest sons of Allee Mahummed, as before mentioned.

The northern provinces of Hindostan had already suffered much from the intestine broils

broils of their rulers, when a new and more destructive convulsion took place, which soon reduced many of them to a state of general desolation.

Soon after the Rohillas had returned from Oude, the *Mahrattas*, encouraged by the debility of the court, and the present discordant state of all the Mussulman powers, invaded the *Doâb* with a considerable army, and spread their ravages over the whole country between the Ganges and the Jumna, until they reached the territories of Nijeeb-al-Dowlah, of whom it may be here necessary to give some account.

This extraordinary man was an Afgan of the *Kummer-Khail* tribe, who had, in his early youth, come from the mountains of Candahâr, to seek his fortune under his uncle, Bisharet Khan. With him he followed the standard of Allee Mahummed, and the uncle dying, succeeded to his command under that adventurer.—Allee Mahummed, on his final establishment in Rohilcund, had

had rewarded his ſervices with a grant of a ſmall diſtrict which forms the northern part of that province.

After Allee Mahummed's death, Nijeeb-al-Dowlah ſtill remained firmly attached to the intereſts of the Rohillas; and in their laſt war with Sefdar Jung, when they took refuge in the hills, he remarkably ſignalized himſelf in their defence; and on ſeveral occaſions, by his valour and good conduct, greatly retarded the approaches of the enemy; in conſequence of which, when affairs were ſettled, he had ſome additions made to his diſtricts; and Doondy Khan beſtowed upon him his eldeſt daughter in marriage.—Thus ſtrengthened and connected, he was joined by a multitude of Afgan freebooters, and by their means poſſeſſed himſelf of all that valuable tract of country ſtretching weſtward from the Ganges to the diſtrict of Siharenpore, along the foot of the hills, and ſouthward almoſt to the gates of Delhi; and as, in in the present distractions of the empire, there were no immediate claimants to dispute his right, he soon established himself in this quarter. From hence he repaired to court, where all ranks and orders of society seemed to be confounded, and every individual, however infamous, was at liberty to raise himself to distinction by the force of his abilities, or the power of his arm.—Here he conducted himself with such address as soon ingratiated him with some of the leading men, and Ghazee-ad-deen, conscious of his inability to dispossess him of the country he had seized, and in hopes of rendering him subservient to his future views, obtained for him from Ahmed Shah a royal grant of all those territories: thus he soon grew into great consequence, and afterwards became a powerful supporter of the Rohilla interests.

On the approach of the *Mahrattas*, as already related, Nijeeb-al-Dowlah collected

lected his forces together, in order to oppose these powerful invaders; but, after some skirmishes, finding he was unable to withstand them in the open field, he threw himself, with the greatest part of his forces, into some strong entrenchments at *Sooker-Tâll* upon the western bank of the Ganges, and wrote to his friends at Kuttâher for assistance; in consequence of which the chiefs immediately dispatched Buxy Sirdar Khan with his forces to Nijeeb-al-Dowlah's aid, and wrote to Suja-al-Dowlah, requiring of him, in the present exigency, a return of those good offices which they had rendered him some months ago; in conformity to which, the Subadâr collected together some of his troops, and advanced by rapid marches towards the scene of action.

In the mean time, a body of Mahrattas crossed the Ganges at a ford near *Hirdewar*, and laid waste all the portion of Nijeeb-al-Dowlah's country which was situated to the eastward of that river; continually eluding,

eluding, by the rapidity of their movements, every attempt of the Rohillas to bring them to action; but on the approach of Suja-al-Dowlah, they thought it moſt adviſeable to retreat. On the junction of the Subadâr of Owde with the Afgans, the whole prepared to paſs the Ganges and attack the Mahrattas in the Doâb; but, on receiving intelligence of this deſign, the latter raiſed the blockade by which they had hitherto confined Nijeeb-al-Dowlah within his intrenchments, and having plundered all the open country, retired towards Agra.—— The Rohillas ſtill remained in the field; but Suja-al-Dowlah, on the Mahrattas going off, returned to Oude.

It was at this period that Ahmed Abdâllee directed his attention a ſecond time towards Hindoſtan.

He had long been checked in his deſigns upon this ſide by Meer Munnoo, who with great valour and good conduct protected for a time the ſhattered remains of the empire

pire towards the *Punjáb.*—Unfortunately, this gallant general was killed by an accident: and the royal army were ſo diſpirited by this event, and fell into ſuch diſorder from the want of a proper leader, that Ahmed Abdâllee with eaſe eſtabliſhed himſelf in all the province of Lahore, took that city with little oppoſition, and obliged the Mogul forces to fall back to Sirhind.

It would be difficult to paint a more diſtreſsful ſcene than what the court at Delhi at this time exhibited. Allumgeer II. the wretched repreſentative of the houſe of Timur, found himſelf ſurrounded by the factions of contending nobles, who, utterly devoid of every ſentiment of loyalty and attachment, ſupported him in the nominal aſſumptions of regal dignity, merely with a view to render him ſubſervient to their ſchemes of ambition; and were ready at any time to take him off by the bowl or the dagger, when it ſhould ſuit their purpoſe.

Soon after the death of Meer Munnoo, this unhappy prince privately invited Ahmed Abdâllee to Delhi, and besought his protection against his own servants.

The Candahâr prince had reasons sufficient to induce him to comply readily with this request. He therefore marched from Lahore with an army of seventy thousand Durânees; and whilst upon his march, he wrote to the sons of Allee Mahummed (whom he had lately set free) and to the other Rohilla chiefs, requiring their assistance in settling the affairs of the empire; and promising them such rewards as, by their means in forwarding his measures, he might be enabled to bestow upon them.—He wrote to the same effect to Nijeeb-al-Dowlah; that chief, however, was constrained from political motives to dissemble, as he held a high office under Ghâzee-ad-deen; and the minister having resolved to march against the *Durânees*, Nijeeb-al-Dowlah joined him, for the present, with his troops; but secretly pledged himself

himſelf to the King (whoſe ſole deſire was to overthrow Ghazee-ad-deen) that he would go ever to Ahmed Abdâllee on the very firſt opportunity; and he even gave that prince private intimation of his deſign. The chiefs in Rohilcund took a more open and decided part in favour of Ahmed Abdâllee. On the receipt of his letters, Fyzoola Khan, with two of his brothers, proceeded to Sirhind, where they found the Candahâr prince; and giving him many valuable preſents, aſſured him of the invariable attachment of the Rohillas to his intereſts.

From Sirhind Ahmed Abdâllee advanced towards Delhi.—Ghazee-ad-deen attempted to retard his progreſs and was preparing to give him battle, when he found himſelf ſuddenly deſerted by Nijeeb-al-Dowlah and his forces, which conſtituted a chief part of his army. The miniſter ſoon perceived the ſnare into which he had fallen; but his abilities enabled him to ward off the ruin intended by it: with a deciſive a decisive promptitude, and a confidence in the honour of his enemy, which are seldom seen in that part of the world, he delivered himself up to the Abdâllee, and soon found means to allay the resentment and conciliate the favour of that prince; mean while, the Abdâllee marched unmolested to Delhi, which city he entered on the eleventh day of September, 1757.

He had here an interview with the Emperor, of whom he demanded a *subsidy* to defray the expence of this expedition, which he professed to have been undertaken entirely at his instigation. The weak monarch gave him authority under his seal to levy a contribution upon this account, to the amount of a *crore* of rupees, on Delhi and the adjacent country; and this exaction being inforced with exceeding severity, some disturbances arose in the course of it, the consequence of which was a dreadful massacre and general pillage of the misera-ble inhabitants; and the unhappy Allumgeer saw the result of the desperate step he had purſued, in the deſtruction of his capital, and the overthrow of the laſt remnant of the Mogul greatneſs.

It were painful to dwell upon ſuch horrid ſcenes: ſuffice it to ſay that, after having permitted his ſoldiers for fifty-ſix days to commit at pleaſure every lawleſs outrage, Ahmed Abdâllee reinſtated Ghazee-ad-deen in his office, delivered the Emperor back into the power of that miniſter, who was now become his implacable enemy, and marched ſouthward againſt the *Jâts*, who had of late erected a powerful eſtabliſhment in the countries about Agra.

On this expedition, Ahmed Abdâllee was accompanied by Hafiz Rahmut with a large body of Rohillas.

Agra was ſtill held in the Emperor's name.—Fazil Khan, the governor, ſhut his gates, and refuſed the Candahâr prince admittance, upon which he beſieged it in form; but the inhabitants, warned by the recent fate of Delhi, ſo well ſeconded the bravery of their governor, that Ahmed Abdâllee, after lying before the place for ſix weeks, found it adviſeable to raiſe the ſiege. He next attacked the Jâts, and having taken many of their ſtrong holds, (which he put into the poſſeſſion of the Rohilla chiefs,) and plundered all the open country round Agra, on the approach of the rainy ſeaſon, he retired into cantonments at Anapſheér, in June, 1758.

During his ſtay at this place, Ahmed Abdâllee, into whoſe hands the preceding events had thrown the whole power of the ſtate, took upon him, under pretence of regulating the affairs of the Mogul government, to give away provinces and depoſe or ſet up rulers at pleaſure: and as the Rohillas had ſo entirely coincided in all his meaſures, he divided among them the diſtricts which he had lately overrun in the *Doâb:* to Nijeeb-al-Dowlah he allotted the Jagheer of Secundna; to Fyzoola Khan, Shikohabâd; and to Sydoola Khan, Jellaſer and Fyrozeabad: and upon Hafiz Rahmut and Doondy Khan he beſtowed the government of *Etáwa*, comprehending all the territory between Agra and Kulpee. It is to be obſerved, however, that the greateſt part of this diſtribution was, for the preſent at leaſt, merely nominal; the Rohillas being as yet in no condition to avail themſelves of it to any great extent.

On the breaking up of the rains, Ahmed Abdâllee proceeded to Delhi, and intended to have ſpent a few weeks in the neighbourhood of that place; but having received, about this time, ſome diſagreeable intelligence from his own country, he ſet off ſuddenly for that quarter.

The unfortunate Emperor was now entirely in the power of his implacable miniſter: Nijeeb-al-Dowlah, in whom alone he could place any confidence, was buſied in ſecuring the diſtricts which had been put in his poſſeſſion by Ahmed Abdâllee; and Ghazee-ad-deen, no longer feeling any check

check from the Candahàr prince, behaved with the utmoſt cruelty to Allumgeer Shah, confined him within certain apartments of his palace, made uſe of his name as an authority for the commiſſion of every enormity, and even endeavoured to ſecure the perſon of the prince, Allee Gohar *, who with difficulty eſcaped from him.

At length the unhappy Allumgeer found an opportunity to write to Ahmed Abdâllee an account of his ſituation, and once more applied to him for relief, to which the Candahâr prince returned a favourable reply, promiſing to ſettle his own affairs, and proceed to Delhi with all poſſible expedition, and threatening Ghazee-ad-deen with the ſevereſt puniſhment. By ſome miſmanagement this letter fell into the miniſter's hands, and he, in revenge of the Emperor's appeal to the Abdâllee, had him aſſaſſinated.

As the prince, Allee Gohar, who was the next heir to the throne, had fled from

* The preſent Emperor.

the machinations of the minister, and at the period of his father's murder, was wandering through the country, and applying to different princes for protection and relief, the empire was for some time without any acknowledged head, and the reign of the house of Timur seemed to be an end.

The Mahrattas had retired to their own country, as before related, and were prevented from undertaking any thing to the northward again, during the stay of Ahmed Abdâllee;—and it was at this juncture that they were induced, from the deranged posture of affairs, and the universal anarchy which seemed to prevail in every department of the Mogul state, to attempt overturning the Mahommedan, and establishing the ancient Hindoo government.

With this view, Bala Row, the Peishwa, levied an immense army, the command of which he designed for his brother, Ragonet Row;—but a dispute arising between them concerning the provision of of the neceſſary ſupplies, Ragonet Row refuſed to undertake the management of the expedition, which was, of conſequence, committed to Mahdo Sidda Sheô, commonly called the Bhao, the ſon of Chimna Jee Apa. As the Peiſhwa abſolutely refuſed to part with any money for the ſupport of the army to be employed in this undertaking, declaring "that a Mahratta army ought always to be able to ſubſiſt itſelf "by plunder," Sidda Sheô firſt turned his arms againſt the Nizâm, who being totally unprepared for any contention with ſuch a prodigious force, was obliged to pay him down a conſiderable ſum, and to render up, by treaty, the countries of Burhan-pore and Mâlava. Sidda Sheô immediately laid theſe countries under contribution, and then marched northward, ſuppoſing that the Muſſulman powers, from their inteſtine diviſions, would become an eaſy prey to ſo great a force *.

 The

* The particulars of the Mahratta tranſactions at Delhi and elſewhere, previous to the battle of Paney- put,

The time which had been neceſſarily occupied in the foregoing preparations, gave the Mahommedans full opportunity for taking the neceſſary meaſures to avert the danger which threatened " *the faith*" ; and they, for a time, forgot their mutual animoſities, and zealouſly united in this common cauſe.

Ahmed Abdàllee, in purſuance of his promiſe to the Emperor Allumgeer, had returned to Gungapore, near Sirhind, where he was joined by Nijeeb-al-Dowlah, and his friends the Rohilla chiefs, with a large body of Afgans ; and he was ſoon after reinforced by the arrival of Suja-al-Dowlah and Ahmed Khan Bungiſh.

The circumſtances of this junction, and the ſubſequent defeat of the Mahrattas, are already well known.—The Mahrattas,

---

put, although ſlightly touched upon by the Rohilla hiſtorian, are here omitted, as irrelevant to our principal object.

contrary

contrary to their uſual rule of conduct in the field, inſtead of carrying on the campaign in that predatory kind of war, to which their numerous bodies of horſe are beſt adapted, ſuffered themſelves to be drawn into a ſituation, from whence they could not by any means be extricated without coming to a deciſive engagement. After ſome diſputes among their chiefs concerning their future operations, they intrenched themſelves in the neighbourhood of Paneyput-Kurnall.—This was the very point at which Ahmed Abdâllee (who acted as generaliſſimo of the united army of the Muſſulmans) had aimed.—The Hindoos were ſurrounded by the Muſſulman armies on every ſide: their ſupplies were all cut off, and their foraging parties deſtroyed; ſo that they were ſoon reduced to the utmoſt diſtreſs.—To add to their perplexity, they were deſerted by Sooraj Mull, who had ſtrongly diſapproved of their intrenching, and foreſeeing the probable conſequence, with an infidelity which ſeems to to be a marking characteriſtick of all the Indian

Indian powers, opened a ſecret negociation with Ahmed Abdâllee; and, by the contrivance of the Muſſulman commander, an attack being directed againſt a diſtant quarter of the Mahratta camp, in the midſt of a very dark night, the above chief found an opportunity, whilſt the attention of his allies was engaged by this manœuvre, to quit his lines unperceived; and paſſing through the Mahommedan army, went off towards Agra, with many thouſands of the Jâts, whom the Mahrattas had perſuaded or compelled to join them. The attack of the Muſſulmans having fully anſwered the only purpoſe intended by it, Ahmed Abdâllee ſent orders to the aſſailants to return into their own lines. The neceſſary conſequence of this order was a retreat, which the Hindoos attributing to a wrong motive, they were filled with ſuch a confidence in their own proweſs as determined them (independent of the preſent diſtreſs of their ſituation) to march out of their intrenchments the next day, and attack their enemies.—This brought on *the*

battle

battle of Paneyput, one of the moſt bloody engagements which has occurred in modern times.

The plain on which this action was fought had been celebrated among the Hindoos for ſome ſignal victories gained upon it by their anceſtors over the barbarians of the north; and the ſtake to be now contended for was of the utmoſt magnitude to both ſides, including in it nothing leſs than the ultimate fate of two rival powers, and the decided ſuperiority or the eventual extirpation of the Muſſulmans in Hindoſtan.

The idea of this being *fortunate ground*, and the preſumption inſpired by the ſuppoſed repulſe of their enemies the preceding night, filled the Hindoos, on the preſent occaſion, with an enthuſiaſm approaching to madneſs. They ruſhed out of their intrenchments without any regular order, and where repulſed by the Mahommedans with prodigious loſs. The defection of the Jâts was not yet certainly known

among

among them, when a large column of horſe, led by the Rohilla commanders, poured down upon them under cover of a cloud of duſt, and forming on the ground which the Jâts had occupied, ſeparated the Mahratta army into two parts; whilſt a body of ſix thouſand Durânnees, who had been detached by Ahmed Abdâllee as ſoon as he diſcovered their intention to engage, having made a rapid circuit of ſome miles, appeared in the rear of their right wing. This decided the fate of the day. The Mahratta right wing being nearly ſurrounded, was entirely cut to pieces; and their left, after many deſperate efforts, having loſt ſeveral of their principal leaders, at length gave way, and a total route enſued. The Muſſulmans purſued them upwards of ſixty miles, and in a ſhort time totally deſtroyed that army which but a few days before had been ſo numerous and formidable.—It is computed that the loſs of the Hindoos upon this occaſion amounted to not leſs than one hundred thouſand men, among whom were their general Sidda

Sheô

Sheô, and Viſwaſs Row, the Peiſhwa's eldeſt ſon; together with the whole of their treaſure, artillery, and baggage*.

Ahmed Abdâllee, ſhortly after this victory, returned to Delhi, where he placed the prince Jewân Bukht, the eldeſt ſon of the heir apparent, Allee Gohar, upon the throne, committing the guardianſhip and ſuperintendence of the government under the young prince, until the return of his father,

* As the Rohilla text is the only authority we have conſulted in our relation of this action, it is not unlikely that it may contain many inaccuracies.—One thing muſt be remarked, which is, the total omiſſion, in it, of the eminent part which Suja-al-Dowlah bore in this memorable event.—It was certainly natural for the national pride of a Rohilla to aſcribe to his own countrymen more than their due portion of merit, and perhaps, to detract from that of Suja-al-Dowlah, whom a perſon of this tribe cannot be ſuppoſed inclined to repreſent in any favourable point of view.—It is, however, but juſtice to obſerve, that all *other* accounts concur in the circumſtance of Suja-al-Dowlah having, by his bravery and activity, rendered the fortune of the day deciſive.

father, into the hands of Nijeeb-al-Dowlah, whom he raised to the office of prime minister, and the dignity of *Ameer-al-Amrah*. The infamous Ghazee-ad-deen, apprehensive of being called to account by the Abdâllee for the murder of the Emperor Allumgeer, had some time before withdrawn himself from all political concerns, and retired to the *Décan*. After settling affairs at Delhi in the best manner that the circumstances of the time would admit, the Candahâr prince returned towards his own country.

The partition of the countries in the *Doâb*, which Ahmed Abdâllee had made the year before, among the Afgan chiefs, could not fail of exciting a war between those powers and the Jâts, who had been the former possessors: but as Nijeeb-al-Dowlah was chiefly concerned in it, and had now all the wealth or force which remained from the ruins of the empire, at his command, the Rohillas, with his assistance, repressed all their attempts to recover

cover their countries, and eſtabliſhed themſelves with every appearance of permanent ſecurity as well here as in their original poſſeſſions in Kuttâher; whilſt Suja-al-Dowlah omitted no means to improve his power and confirm his independence in the province of Oude.

In this diſpoſition of things, the jarring intereſts of Suja-al-Dowlah, the Rohillas, and other Muſſulman chiefs in theſe provinces, who had totally thrown off all farther dependence upon the Mogul government, (which, in fact, at this time, ceaſed to exiſt) and now held their dominions in their own right by the tenure of the ſword, might have continued to be pretty well balanced, perhaps, for ſome years;—but, in the mean time, a power ſprung up equally formidable and unexpected; the ſuperior influence of which ſoon wrought a great change in the general political ſyſtem.

The Engliſh, having ſurmounted incredible

dible hardſhips and difficulties in Bengal, had been led, from motives of immediate ſelf-preſervation, to take ſuch ſteps as ended in the acquiſition of the complete and uncontrolled dominion of that and all the neighbouring dependent provinces. The particulars which led to ſo important a revolution are foreign to this narrative: ſuffice it to ſay, that on their breach with the Nabob Meer Coſſim Allee Khan, the Britiſh commanders defeated and purſued him out of Behâr, conſtraining him to ſeek refuge in the neighbouring province of Oude.—Sujà-al-Dowlah was not a little alarmed at the rapid progreſs and unexampled ſucceſs of theſe new neighbours.—At the moment, however, when their good fortune ſeemed to have operated deciſively in their favour, he learned that a dreadful mutiny had broke out in the Engliſh army, and that a general deſertion threatened its annihilation, whilſt he knew that their lately-acquired dominion was ſtill involved in the confuſion and derangement incident to recent conqueſt.—Ever watchful, as he

was,

was, to ſeize any occaſion that might offer for his own aggrandizement, and the enlargement of his dominion; he conceived the preſent a happy opportunity at once to relieve his fears and gratify his ambition, by poſſeſſing himſelf of the Bengal provinces.—Theſe ſentiments, added to the influence and treaſure of the expelled Nabob, determined him, without even a ſhadow of provocation, to make head againſt the Engliſh. He accordingly collected all the forces he could muſter, and with a ſhort-ſighted and heedleſs temerity marched towards Patna, on pretence of acting under the orders of the prince Allee Gohar (who had ſome time before thrown himſelf on his protection) and reſtoring Coſſim Allee Khan to the Muſnud of Bengal.—In this expedition he was joined by a conſiderable body of Rohillas under Enâit Khan, the ſon of Hafiz Rahmut.—Being repulſed in the ſkirmiſh of Pitchee-Pehârey, and afterwards totally defeated at Buxar, he fled to Fyzabad, and hearing of the march of a detachment of Engliſh troops towards

 Lucknow

Lucknow, he took refuge in Rohilcund. He was hoſpitably received and entertained at Barellee by Doondee Khan.—Here he made many attempts to procure the aſſiſtance of the Rohilla chiefs againſt the Engliſh; but they, terrified by the recent fate of Coſſim Allee Khan, and Suja-al-Dowlah's ill ſucceſs, would not venture to take any part in his favour: he at laſt, however, prevailed on Hafiz Rahmut to join him with a body of three thouſand Afgans, and being farther reinforced by a ſmall army of Mahrattas under Mulhar Row, was encouraged to try his fortune once more in the field againſt the Engliſh.—He advanced into the *Doab*, and made ſome attempts againſt the troops under General Carnac, and was again defeated.—Hopeleſs of ſucceſs, and deſerted by a great part of his troops, Suja-al-Dowlah at length determined to throw himſelf upon the generoſity of his enemies, and ſoon after came into the Britiſh general's camp. Theſe occurrences led to the celebrated "*treaty of Allehabad.*" By this treaty Suja-al-Dowlah was reinſtated in his original dominion of Oude, and every other right he enjoyed previous to the war, except the dominion of the provinces of Korah and Allehabâd, which form the ſouthern part of the *Doáb*. —Theſe diſtricts had been preſented by Ahmed Abdâllee (in his general partition of the *Daáb* among the Afgan chiefs) to Sydoola Khan, who, being ſenſible of his inability to ſubdue or hold them, as they lay at a conſiderable diſtance from Rohilcund, made them over to Suja-al-Dowlah, and that prince had ſeized the forts of Kurra and Allehabad, and ſome other ſtrong holds in theſe territories, but had not yet been able to eſtabliſh himſelf in perfect poſſeſſion of the country, when his unprovoked war with the Engliſh drew his attention from every other object. The prince Allee Gohar, whom we have ſo often mentioned, on the defeat of Suja-al-Dowlah at Buxar, had thrown himſelf upon the protection of the conquerors, and as ſucceſſor to his father, Allumgeer, had aſſumed the title of Emperor, under the name of *Shah Aulum.*

lum.—This prince was a party in the before-mentioned treaty.—The Engliſh, by the ſucceſs of their arms, had already obtained full and entire poſſeſſion of the province of Bengal, and its dependencies:—it was, however, deemed neceſſary (from what poſſible motive of reaſon or policy we cannot take upon us to judge) to obtain an *oſtenſible* claim to the tenure of them, on the preſent occaſion, by procuring from an impotent monarch, who was himſelf a fugitive and a dependant on the Engliſh for the very *crown* and *title* which he had aſſumed,—a commiſſion to the Company of the *Dewannée* of the Bengal provinces; and the Emperor had, in return, an annual *penſion* or tribute * ſettled upon him, to be paid out of the Bengal revenues, and was guaranteed in the

* The writer is not informed by what appellation this was ſpecified in the treaty of Allehabad.—It is denominated in the MS. *Salleeâna Nizzerâna*, which may be rendered, "Annual gratuity," a general appellation which does not imply *poſitive right.*

poſſeſſion

poſſeſſion of the provinces of Korah and Allehabâd, where he reſided for ſome time after.

Although theſe tranſactions were not immediately connected with the hiſtory of the Rohillas, yet, as they in their conſequences led to events of the moſt material importance with reſpect to that tribe, it was neceſſary to take ſome particular notice of them here. It is alſo proper to remark that about the period of which we have been treating, the new Emperor advanced Suja-al-Dowlah to the office of the *Vizaret*, an appointment, however, which the preſent ſtate of the ſovereign rendered merely nominal.

On Suja-al-Dowlah ſurrendering himſelf to the Engliſh, Hafiz Rahmut and his followers returned to Rohilcund, and thither we ſhall now accompany them.

Abdoola Khan being exceedingly diſguſted at the iniquitous conduct of his guardians, had retired to Oojânee, (as before observed)* and there, putting on the habit of a *Dirveish*, or *Fakeer*, employed himself in distributing the whole of the income arising from the lands allotted for his support, in alms to the poor; and, in conformity to the practice of the order of which he professed himself a member, affected to cherish snakes and other noxious animals, by one of which he was bit in the arm, and almost instantly expired, in August, 1761.—About three years after that event, Sydoola Khan, during the absence of Hafiz Rahmut, was seized with a consumption, and died in 1764; and only *two* of Allee Mahummed's children now remained alive; viz. Fyzoola Khan and Mahummed-Yâr Khan.

These are the only events of note which occurred in Rohilcund during the space of seven years; to wit, from the battle of Paneyput to the second incursion of the

---

* Page 120.

Mahrattas

Mahrattas into the Doâb. During this interval they had no enemies to interrupt their tranquillity from without; and, although the injuſtice of the guardians gave riſe to frequent jealouſies and diſputes, yet the vigorous adminiſtration of the chiefs who had uſurped the government, preſerved the country in a tolerable degree of internal harmony; but we have no documents from which we might enter into a more minute deſcription of the domeſtick management or political intrigues which occupied their attention within this period; as all that the Rohilla narrator remarks upon it is—"The Afgan *Sirdars*, being freed "from the vexatious interruptions of the "marauders of the *Deccan*," (the *Mahrattas*) "by their chaſtiſement at Paneyput, "and allaying the ferments of the diſcor-"dant and the factious by the wiſdom of "their auſpicious councils, paſſed ſeven "years in harmony and eaſe."

The Mahrattas had ſuffered ſo very ſeverely by their defeat at Paneyput, that ſome years paſſed away before they would venture to do any thing of conſequence again in the northern provinces. At length, having reſolved to deprive the Afgans of thoſe countries, which, by the favour of Ahmed Abdâllee, they held in the Doâb, Mahdo Jee Sindea, (the ſucceſſor of Malhar Row) Toke Jee Holcar, and other chiefs, croſſed the Jumna with a conſiderable body of troops, in the year 1769.

Nijeeb-al-Dowlah, who continued to manage affairs at Delhi in the abſence of the Kiug, as nominal miniſter, on hearing this intelligence, and finding that the Mahrattas were in great force, made a merit of neceſſity, and joined theſe marauders in their depredations againſt the *Jâts*; and at the ſame time a negociation was opened through his mediation between the Afgan chiefs and Mahratta commanders, reſpecting the ſurrender of thoſe diſtricts in the Doâb to which the latter laid claim. Doondee Khan, who had never much concerned himſelf in the care of theſe diſtricts,

was

was willing to come to an amicable compromise with the Mahrattas; and, in a council of the chiefs which was held on the occasion, said,—"I have no ability to "meet the chiefs of the south in the "doubtful strife of war:—if they will, "from a desire of peace and amity, per-"mit me to retain the district of Shikko-"habâd alone, I shall acknowledge their "kindness; but if not, I shall lift my "hands from these possessions altogether." ——Hafiz Rahmut, who was present, and whose possessions in the Doâb were valuable and productive, with a characteristick boldness, laying his hand upon his scymitar, replied,——"Whilst I "live, I shall hope; nor will I suffer "an ill-timed and groundless despon-"dence to deprive me of those favours "which, with the help of God, I re-"ceived from the illustrious Abdâllee!" —On the council breaking up, Doondee Khan went off to his own district, and Hafiz Rahmut and his party proceeded to take such steps as shewed them determined to oppose the views of the Mahrattas with all their might. For this purpose they entered into a treaty with Ahmed Khan Bungish, promising, in lieu of his support, to cede to him some of those lands which lay contigious to the Ferrochabad government.—To the first overtures made on this business to Ahmed Khan they received a favourable answer; and relying upon the aid which they should derive from this alliance, a considerable body of the Rohillas marching down to Sandee, crossed the Ganges at Futty Ghurr. Hafiz Rahmut, however, had not deliberated on this occasion with his usual foresight and sagacity. —Ahmed Khan Bungish, whose country lay open to the inroads of the Mahrattas, was fearful of exposing himself to their indignation; and, notwithstanding his reply to the requisitions of the Rohillas, delayed, on a variety of pretexts, to take any decided part against them; and many of the Rohillas themselves being little interested concerning the retention of territories, from which the immediate posses-

sors

ſors alone reaped any advantage, became diſſatisfied and mutinous; ſo that, after ſome months trifling and fruitleſs operation, Hafiz found himſelf obliged to give up the fort of *Etâwa*, and the ſurrounding country, to the Mahrattas, and retired beyond the Ganges.

Perhaps their loſs of territory in the Doâb, by circumſcribing their line of defence, might have added to the real ſtrength of the Rohillas, inſtead of diminiſhing it: but the Afgan intereſts, ſhortly after this, ſuffered an irreparable blow in the death of Nijeeb-al-Dowlah, who, from the period of his ſucceeding Ghazee-ad-deen in the office of prime miniſter, had continued for the remainder of his life to ſupport the laſt wretched fragment of the fallen empire at Delhi, with a firmneſs which would in happier times have inſured him the approbation and applauſe of mankind; and although, in this laſt ſcene of it, the urgency of preſent neceſſity conſtrained him to take a part with

with their opponents, yet, as well from natural relation as from political connection, he had always been warmly attached to the Afgan party. — He left a ſon named Zabita Khan, who ſucceeded his father in the poſſeſſion of his territories in the northern part of Rohilcund and the *Doâb.*

The Rohilla confederacy likewiſe ſuffered much at this time by the death of Doondee Khan, who had, along with Hafiz Rahmut, been appointed by Allee Mahummed joint guardian to his children. His character ſtood high among thoſe of his tribe, for generoſity of ſpirit, and gallantry in war—inſomuch, that they aſſert, that the acquiſition of Rohilla independence in Kuttâher may, in a great meaſure, be aſcribed to the popularity of his manners and the prudence of his councils.—— Having attained the age of ſeventy years, he died in Biſſoolee of an apoplexy.—He left three ſons, Mahboola Khan, Fittahoola Khan, and Azeemoola Khan, who divided the diſtricts of Moradabad and Biſſoolee

(which

(which had fallen to the lot of their father in the uſurpation of the territory by the guardians) among themſelves.—Not long after this Ahmed Khan Bungiſh died at Ferrochabad, leaving the inheritance of his poſſeſſions to his ſon Muzziffer Jung.

The expulſion of the Rohillas from the Doab, and the utter extinction of the Muſſulman conſequence at Delhi, in the death of Nijeeb-al-Dowlah, removed every obſtruction to the execution of thoſe ſchemes which the Mahrattas had at this time planned for extending their dominion and confirming their power in the capital of the empire. They accordingly took poſſeſſion of Delhi, and wrote to the Emperor Shah Aulum, who then reſided under the protection of the Engliſh at Allehabad, holding forth to him the moſt flattering propoſals of reinſtating him in the ancient ſeat of government, and reſtoring him to the dignity of his anceſtors, if he would forſake his preſent friends, and aſſume the reins of imperial authority at Delhi.

The ſituation of this prince at Allehabad, as a penſioner of the Engliſh, owing not only his preſent nominal dignity, but perhaps even his exiſtence to their protection and ſupport, however mortifying it might be to his pride, yet was certainly preferable to any advantage he could expect to derive from throwing himſelf upon the Mahrattas, who being the hereditary enemies of his family and religion, could not be ſuppoſed to feel any attachment to his perſon; and in fact, only wanted to make him the tool of their own deſigns.— He was ſenſible that his relinquiſhing the protection of the Engliſh muſt neceſſarily be attended with the loſs of his annual ſtipend, which was drawn from the revenues of the Bengal Provinces; as the ſtate of circulation of ſpecie in the empire was not now by any means the ſame as it had been, whilſt the court and the capital flouriſhed in the vigour of the Mogul

Mogul Government.—In former times, when the lower provinces uſed to yield a regular tribute to the Emperors (which they have not done for above half a century paſt) the greateſt part of it was remitted by bills upon Delhi and Lahore, for the payment of which ſufficient funds were there ſupplied in the ſale and conſumption of the rich manufactures of Bengal; in fact, if it had not been ſo, no tribute could ever have been remitted; and when the depredations of Nadir Shah, and a variety of other circumſtances, contributed, by impoveriſhing the court, to ſtop the vent for theſe commodities in this quarter, the ſtoppage of the tribute was a neceſſary and inevitable conſequence, independent of any actual defection on the part of the Nabobs of Bengal; as it was utterly impoſſible that the ſame, or indeed any conſiderable ſum, could ever be continued to be tranſmitted in *caſh*, from a country of which gold and ſilver form no part of the natural products.—All theſe circumſtances Shah Aulum muſt have been well aware of, of, and knew that the Englifh could not, in common prudence, continue to tranfmit to him, whilft at fo great a diftance, large fums in fpecie (the only mode of remittance now remaining,) which muft be at once a fatal drain to the countries from whence they were taken, and an affiftance to the Mahrattas, whofe views were avowedly inimical to all their allies. — He was however induced, by the fuggeftions of a childifh vanity, and the idle hope of reftoring the Mogul empire to its former luftre, to leave Korah (a city in the neighbourhood of Allehabad, where he then refided) and, contrary to the advice of all his real friends and well-wifhers, proceeded to Delhi in the year 1770.

On his arrival at the capital, the Mahrattas enthroned him with the ufual ceremonies, (which, in fuch circumftances, could only be termed a *mockery* of royalty,) and caufed him to iffue fuch *firmans* and grants as beft coincided with their views: and the Shah, as a reward for their pretended

tended fidelity to his cauſe, made over to them, by a formal inſtrument, the provinces of Korah and Allehabâd, and alſo every territory to the eaſt of Delhi without exception; thus giving them an unreſtrained commiſſion to extend their ravages into all the countries on each ſide of the Ganges.

In order to underſtand the deſigns and ſubſequent operations of the Mahrattas, it may be neceſſary here to obſerve that the river Ganges, which forms the natural boundary of Rohilcund to the weſt, is fordable only within the compaſs of that territory, and no where lower down, ſo that the province of Oude, which lies to the ſouthward, is invulnerable to thoſe marauders, excepting through the former country, as their numerous bodies of horſe have no ſure means of advance and retreat but by the ſhallows of the Ganges during the dry ſeaſon; their deſultory method of carrying on war not ſuiting with the conſtruction of bridges, and other tedious and expenſive military works, (ſuch as might give them a command of the paſſage of unfordable rivers,) nor their mode of fighting calculated for the defence of them.

On taking a view of the extenſive theatre of action which now lay before them, the Mahratta commanders perceived that, as the diſtricts of Korah and Allehabâd were in ſome meaſure defended by a conſiderable body of Britiſh troops lying in that neighbourhood, their moſt adviſeable plan of operation would be to direct their firſt attacks againſt the territories of the Rohillas, ſo as through them to find an inroad to the dominions of Suja-al-Dowlah, where their principal views were directed.

Under colour, therefore, of the grants which they had procured or exacted from the Emperor, when the ſeaſon for action arrived, the Mahrattas took the field *,

* Dec. 1771.

and

and firſt turned their arms againſt Zabita Khan, who held the poſſeſſions bequeathed to him by his father, in the ſame independent manner as the other Afgan chiefs. Zabita Khan, little prepared for ſuch an attack, threw himſelf with what forces he could muſter into the intrenchments which had formerly been conſtructed by Nijeeb-al-Dowlah at *Sooker-Tall** ; the enemy, however, being provided with ſome heavy artillery, preſſed ſo cloſely upon him, that he was ſoon conſtrained to evacuate his lines, and to make a precipitate retreat over the Ganges, under cover of the night. The Mahrattas, two days after, paſſed that river by the ford at Corrimboſsgaut, in purſuit of him; and followed him ſo cloſely that he fled towards the hills above Lolldong in the utmoſt conſternation, leaving his family and valuable effects at the fort of Pattergúrr or Nijeebabad, the capital of his territory beyond the Ganges, which the enemy preſently

* Page 134.

attacked and carried without difficulty. Here they ſeized Zabita Khan's mother, his wives, two brothers, and four of his children, and ſent them off to their camp on the weſt of the Ganges: they alſo plundered this city, and all the ſurrounding towns and villages, with their uſual avidity; and with a ſavage ferocity, directed perhaps by religious prejudices more than by a wanton ſpirit of deſolation, deſtroyed moſt of the moſques and other publick buildings, and in particular defaced the monument of Nijeeb-al-Dowlah, a piece of remarkably curious and coſtly workmanſhip.

The Rohilla chiefs, who appear on this occaſion to have been totally unprepared for reſiſtance, were ſtruck with terror at the unexpected progreſs of the Mahrattas; and following the example of Zabita Khan, retired with their families and treaſures into the foreſts of Gungapore, where they ſtrongly intrenched themſelves; and continued ſhut up in that manner near four months: in the mean time, the Mahrattas ranged

ranged at pleaſure throughout the whole country, plundering, burning and deſtroying all before them.

At length Suja-al-Dowlah, alarmed by the danger which threatened his dominions, advanced with ſome Engliſh battallions under the command of Brigadier General Sir Robert Barker, (then commander in chief of the Bengal army,) to Shawbâd on the borders of his territories; and from hence Captain Harper (a gentleman who for ſome time commanded a corps in the province of Oude, and whoſe knowledge of the politicks of theſe countries, was remarkably accurate and extenſive) was deputed to the Rohilla chiefs, in order to open with them a negotiation with reſpect to ſuch meaſures as might tend to the effectual expulſion of the Mahrattas from their territories.—Hafiz Rahmut, on this gentleman's approach, ventured out of his intrenchments, and proceeded with him to the camp of Suja-al-Dowlah, with whom he had an interview on the banks of the Ramgunga. The particulars of the conference are not related; but the event of it was a treaty * of mutual defence and co-operation between the Rohillas and the Subadâr of Oude, and an engagement by Hafiz-Rahmut, on the part of the former (expreſſly comprehending in the obligation of it *all* the Sirdars of Rohilcund) to pay to Suja-al-Dowlah the ſum of *forty lacks* of rupees, for his aſſiſtance in repelling the common enemy, and reſtoring the ſeveral chiefs to their poſſeſſions, in whatever manner this might be effected; and of which *ten lacks* were to be payable immediately, and the remainder by inſtallments †; and there was a particular clauſe in this agreement, that if the Mahrattas ſhould, on account of the lateneſs of the ſeaſon ‡, retire for

* See Appendix, No. 1.

† See Appendix, No. 2.

‡ This negotiation took place in June 1772.—The rains generally commence in theſe northern countries, in the latter end of that month, or the beginning of July, and end in October; but the great rivers are not fordable until December.

the

the preſent, the force and meaning of it were to extend, in every reſpect, to the year enſuing. This treaty, and agreement, in order to give them greater validity and effect in the minds of the contracting parties, were executed and ſworn to in the preſence of the Britiſh commander in chief, and counterſigned by him.

"It is here neceſſary to remark," ſays the Rohilla hiſtorian, "that nothing except a weakneſs of judgement from his "advanced age, or a decree of unerring "providence hanging over him for his "injuſtice to the children of his friend, "could ever have led Hafiz Rahmut to "enter into this raſh and impolitick treaty, "by which he threw the Afgans upon "the protection of aliens, and with his "own hand ratified the inſtrument of his "future ruin."

The ſeaſon being ſo far advanced, nothing of material conſequence occurred after this tranſaction.—The Mahrattas retired unmolested to Delhi, and the Rohillas returned to their respective homes, which, especially in the northern districts, presented them with scenes of the most deplorable desolation.—Suja-al-Dowlah returned to Fyzabad, leaving a few troops cantoned at Sandee for the remainder of the season.

Soon after the retreat of the Mahrattas, Buxy Sirdâr Khan, having contracted a fever in the Gungapore woods, died at a very advanced age; and the following character of him (literally taken from the original) may not, perhaps, be unacceptable to our readers:—"For ninety fortunate years Sirdâr Khan lived in this "vale of wretchedness and sorrow:—he "was an holy and religious person:—"from the day of mature discernment "to the last aspiration of mortal existence, "he was daily seen in the congregations "of the mosques, and in the assemblies "of the pious: he was a man just in his "sentiments, and upright in his deal-

"ings;

" ings: he was not, like others of his " tribe, a violator of the ties of friend- " ſhip, or an oppreſſor of the helpleſs; " and excepting the due returns of the " revenue, he took not from the indigent " labourer, or the uſeful tiller of the " ground, a ſingle exaction.—He retained " his faculties to the laſt moment of his " life; and previous to the final departure " of that immortal ſpark which connects " the *human* with the *divine* exiſtence, " whilſt his reaſon was yet alive to the " concerns of this tranſitory ſtate, he " made an equitable diſtribution of the " bleſſings he enjoyed from providence a- " mong his heirs," &c.

Ahmed Khan and Meer Mahummed Khan, the Buxy's two eldeſt ſons, quarrelling concerning the diviſion of their father's country, raiſed a diſturbance which tended greatly to inflame ſome diſcords already prevailing in Rohilcund.

Ahmed Khan, being the ſenior, appealed

pealed to Hafiz Rahmut, who decided in his favour; upon which Meer Mahummed raised troops, and attempted to possess himself of the district of Ahrat (which had been a part of his father's assumed estates) by force: but Futtee-Khan Khansaman met him on the banks of the *Soot Nulla*, totally routed the insurgents, and took Mahummed prisoner.

This insurrection was not yet quelled, when another of a more capital and dangerous nature arose; and Hafiz Rahmut, who had unjustly usurped the rights of those children whom his friend had committed to his guardianship and protection, was doomed to see his own son rise up in rebellion against him.

Enâit Khan, the eldest son of Hafiz Rahmut, had always exhibited marks of a quarrelsome and turbulent disposition; and now, on some trifling difference with his father, raised a body of three thousand of his friends and followers, and surprising the

the fort of Baréllee, ſhut the gates againſt him, declaring his reſolution to hold that diſtrict in future as his own. Hafiz Rahmut, aware that uſing open force againſt his ſon might raiſe diſturbances deſtructive to Baréllee and the neighbouring country, retired to Peeleabête, from whence he wrote to all the other chiefs requiring their aſſiſtance to cruſh this rebellion. On the troops being collected in conſequence of this ſummons, the wily chief, in order to draw his ſon from Baréllee, had recourſe to a ſtratagem perfectly conſiſtent with the duplicity of his character; cauſing a grant to be drawn out, in the name of Enâit Khan, of the diſtrict of Selimpore, which he ſent to him with a letter —— "aſſuring him of his forgiveneſs; "taking blame to himſelf for a deficiency "of parental indulgence, and deſiring him "to go and take poſſeſſion of the above "lands, which he hoped would be con"ſidered by him as ſufficient preſent pro"viſion; and promiſing to reward his "obedience in the ampleſt manner." This artifice

artifice was attended with the desired effect. In a few days Enâit Khan and his followers left Barellee, intending to proceed to Selimpore. Hafiz Rahmut immediately detached a select body of troops in order to seize his son, which after a slight skirmish was effected. When the unfortunate and misguided youth was taken, his father declared his resolution to put him to death, but was persuaded to adopt the scarce more lenient measure of banishing him out of Rohilcund, without any means of subsistence.—Enâit Khan, thus left destitute, went to Suja-al-Dowlah, and after remaining at Fyzabad near twelve months, being reduced to extreme want, returned in despair to Rohilcund. His father positively refused him admittance into Barellee, and he returned to a neighbouring village, where he shortly after died of a broken heart, amidst all the misery of too late repentance and unavailing remorse; — thus," says the Rohilla narrator, " was the parental imprecation amply " fulfilled in him; Hafiz Rahmut, three "different times during his rebellion, "having gone to the Mofque and prayed "aloud, faying, *Caufe the cup of his life,* "*O God! to overflow whilft yet in his youth,* "*fo that no fruit may ever fpring from that* "*inaufpicious branch; and never let me be* "*expofed to the fhame of again beholding* "*his face.*"

In addition to this, and fimilar domeftick difturbances, the defection of Zabita Khan contributed not a little to weaken the power of the Afgans at this period.—His family having been carried off from Pattergûrr, as already related, he applied to Suja-al-Dowlah, intreating him to intercede with Mahda Jee Sindhea, the Mahratta commander, for their releafe.—Suja-al-Dowlah accordingly directed his minifter, Elitch Khan, who was then at Delhi, to make the proper applications upon this fubject, and the requeft was granted on condition that Zabita Khan fhould come over to the Mahrattas, which

he

he accordingly did, in Auguſt, A. D. 1772.

Mahda Jee Sindhea, ſoon after this, proceeded to Poona by the route of Jeynagûr, being called thither by ſome late diſputes between Mahda Row Nirraen, the Peiſhwa, and his uncle, Ragonet Row, which were likely to occaſion diſturbances in the Dêcan.—He left the command of the army to the Mahratta generals, Toko Jee Holcar, and Beyſa Jee Pundit, who, as the ſeaſon fit for action approached, determined to march once more into Rohilcund.

The Mahrattas, on firſt taking the field, in November, 1772, as the Ganges was not yet fordable, moved ſome way down the *Doáb*, with an apparent view of commencing their operations in that country: but, underſtanding that they were likely to meet with effectual oppoſition, upon their ſpies bringing them intelligence that the Ganges had become fordable, they ſuddenly

denly turned, and directed their route to Ramghaut.

From hence the Mahratta commanders (merely as a pretext for their future proceedings) ſent letters to the Rohilla chiefs, demanding payment of the bonds for fifty lacks of rupees, which they had ſome years ago given to Sefdar Jung*, and which had been transferred by him to Mulhar Row.

The chiefs, inſtead of returning any explicit anſwer to theſe requiſitions, aſſembled their forces at a place about fifteen miles diſtant from Ramghaut, and from thence detached a choſen body under the command of Ahmed Khan, (who had ſucceeded Sirdar Khan in the office of *Buxy*) with directions to guard the ford at Ramghaut, and to ſeize all the boats on that part of the river.

The Buxy accordingly marched, but inſtead of following his inſtructions, by

* Page 113.

which

which he would, at all events, have conſtrained the enemy to ſeek a paſſage much higher up, contented himſelf with throwing a part of his forces into a ſmall fort which commanded the road from the ghaut, or ford, into the country, but was not ſo ſituated as to defend the paſſage over the river. Whatever other meaſures he might have intended to purſue, it would appear that he did not adopt them with ſufficient celerity; as Holcar found means to effect a paſſage for his army early the next morning, his cavalry fording at the uſual place, and his infantry and rocket-men being tranſported in boats (many of which they found at hand, notwithſtanding the injunctions given to the Buxy) a little lower down:—and the next day he attacked the Buxy in the fort, and ſoon obliged him to ſurrender, and give up all his artillery and ammunition.——From hence the victorious marauders proceeded to Sumbull, and plundered all the country between that city and Moradabâd;—but they were not long unoppoſed.

It

It has been already ſaid, that the unfortunate and impotent Emperor, Shah Aulum, on deſerting his protectors, and undertaking his romantick expedition to Delhi, thereby throwing himſelf into the power of the Mahrattas, was compelled to grant *firmans*, making over to them the provinces of Korah and Allehabad *. —Some of their motions, before they proceeded to Rohilcund, having indicated an intention on their part to take poſſeſſion of theſe territories, it was judged expedient by the Britiſh government to march a body of troops that way, to be at hand, to protect them, if neceſſary;—our ally, the Vizier, being greatly apprehenſive of the conſequences, ſhould the Mahrattas be permitted to eſtabliſh themſelves ſo very near to him. Accordingly, the firſt brigade of the Engliſh army, then ſtationed at Dinapore, took the field in the beginning of A. D. 1773, under the command of Brigadier-general Sir Robert Barker, and marched into the province of Owde, from whence a detachment was ſent to

 garriſon

* Page 171.

garriſon the fort of Allehabad, and another to occupy the lines at Cawnpore, in order to ſecure the paſſage of the Ganges, ſhould there be occaſion to croſs that river, for the purpoſe of covering thoſe countries which were apprehended to be the object of the Mahrattas' deſigns. As ſoon, however, as intelligence was received of the Mahrattas having marched to Ramghaut, with a view to renew their attacks upon Rohilcund, the combined armies of the Engliſh and Suja-al-Dowlah advanced towards that country by rapid marches, and arrived at Shawbad at the period when Toko Jee croſſed the Ganges, and defeated the Rohillas under the Buxy, as before mentioned.

The Engliſh, immediately after this affair, proceeded to Ramghaut, and had nearly ſurpriſed a body of four thouſand Mahratta horſe whilſt fording the Ganges at the Ghaut of Gurrickpore, about five miles below that place, in order to reinforce their friends on that ſide: the greateſt

greateſt part of them was in the middle of the river, when the Britiſh army came in ſight, upon which they ſuddenly returned, and marched up the weſtern bank, towards Ramghaut, (where Beyſa Jee was encamped with part of the Mahratta army and all their artillery and heavy baggage) whilſt the Britiſh and Vizier's troops continued their route along the oppoſite ſhore, until they arrived at Aſſidpore, within ſight of Beyſa Jee's encampment.—Here the Mahrattas commenced a cannonade againſt the Engliſh; but this was ſoon anſwered by the latter with ſuch effect as preſently ſilenced their artillery, and obliged their whole army to change their ground with ſome precipitation.

The conduct of Hafiz Rahmut and the other Rohilla chiefs, during theſe tranſactions, had exhibited great duplicity; inſomuch that the Britiſh general was not without apprehenſion of ſome colluſion between them and the Mahrattas; and theſe ſuſpicions were increaſed by their ſo long delaying to join him with their forces.—The truth was, that Hafiz Rahmut, unwilling, however able he might be, to take upon himſelf the entire fulfilment of the engagement which he had entered into with Suja-al-Dowlah the preceding year, was deſirous, if he could not altogether evade it, at all events to bear as little as poſſible of the burden; and he had already applied to the other chiefs, endeavouring to convince them of the neceſſity of their aſſiſting him in the diſcharge of the obligation which had been agreed to by him for their common benefit. His remonſtrances, however, were attended with no effect: ſome declared that he had no right to bind them to ſuch a condition,—whilſt the majority ridiculed the idea of any treaty whatever being held obligatory upon the contracting parties, where it could either be infringed with benefit, or broken without danger.—Many, indeed, were not altogether without a ſuſpicion that if Hafiz Rahmut ſhould obtain their ſubſidies in this behalf, he would convert the money

to

to his own uſe, and ſtill endeavour to break his contract with the Vizier, ſo that they would remain as liable to be involved in a quarrel with that power on this account as ever; and they unanimouſly adviſed Hafiz Rahmut, in caſe he ſhould be again preſſed by the Vizier on this ſubject, to protract the final adjuſtment of it on various pretences, to amuſe him with deluſive hopes, and to truſt to future events to extricate him, without expence, from his obligation.—Hafiz did, in effect, adopt this laſt plan, which was much more conſonant to his own ideas of political management than any other; and determined, in caſe the Mahrattas ſhould attempt a ſecond irruption into Rohilcund, to avoid ſoliciting the aid of his former protectors, an interview with whom would inevitably lead to demands which he was now reſolved not to comply with; nor was he without hopes of being able (for he had now complete warning of the enemy's deſigns) to defend the paſſages of the Ganges with the Rohilla forces alone. It was with this view that, on the approach of the Mahrattas towards Ramghaut, he detached the Buxy to guard the fords as already mentioned; and had that officer done his duty, it is probable that Hafiz might not have been disappointed in his expectations, and that the Mahrattas might have met with an effectual check, without any immediate necessity of calling upon the Vizier for his assistance. The mismanagement or treachery of the Buxy, however, opening a way for the invaders, suggested another idea to him, by which he might at once avoid *their* violence, and secure himself against any disagreeable consequences from his non-compliance with the Vizier's demands.—This was no less than to enter into a confederacy with the Mahrattas themselves!—by which they were to obtain, under certain restrictions, a permanent settlement in the country, on engaging to defend the Rohillas against "all "their enemies;"—and he actually employed emissaries privately to negotiate this desperate proposal with the Mahratta commanders:—

manders:—but all his ſchemes were fruſtrated by the rapid and unwiſhed-for advance of the allied army, and Hafiz Rahmut found himſelf, by his own crooked and temporizing policy, entangled in a labyrinth of perplexity and diſtreſs. Yet, even at this time, when the enemy, notwithſtanding his ſecret overtures to them, were plundering and laying waſte all the more defenceleſs parts of the country, he endeavoured to procraſtinate his junction with Suja-al-Dowlah as long as poſſible: —at length, finding that the allies had already advanced into the heart of the Rohilla territories, and underſtanding that they were fully aware of his treacherous proceedings, and had even reſolved to attack him, ſhould he confirm the ſuſpicions his conduct had excited by any longer delay, he collected his forces, and joined Suja-al-Dowlah the next day after the cannonade between the Engliſh and Beyſa Jee *. Some days after that event, as the

* Page 189.

Mahratta army was now divided, part of it being ſtill at Sumbull in Rohilcund under Toko Jee, and the remainder under Beyſa Jee, to the weſtward of the Ganges, it was determined to attack them in both quarters at the ſame time.——With this view the Britiſh troops forded the river at Ramghaut, whilſt Suja-al-Dowlah and Hafiz Rahmut prepared to advance with their united forces againſt Toko Jee.——Beyſa Jee, when he heard of the approach of the brigade, decamped in the utmoſt hurry and confuſion, and went off to the diſtance of forty miles in a ſingle march. From ſome ſuſpicions which Suja-al-Dowlah ſtill entertained of Hafiz Rahmut, the other part of the concerted operation was not executed by him;—but the Engliſh, recroſſing the Ganges the next day after the flight of Beyſa Jee, proceeded towards Sumbull; upon which Toko Jee retreated to *Póot*, a town upon the Ganges, about fifty miles above Ramghaut, and croſſed the river at that place on a bridge of boats, which he afterwards deſtroyed.——The

Mahratta army made ſome movements which indicated an intention of again croſſing into Rohilcund at Corrimboſsghaut, a conſiderable diſtance higher up the river; but the brigade, advancing by rapid marches to that place, prevented them, whilſt the Vizier with his troops guarded all the fords at Ramghaut and the neighbourhood; and as the hot ſeaſon approached, and the Ganges began to be ſwelled by the melting of the ſnows on the northern mountains, they were conſtrained for the preſent to relinquiſh all thoughts of renewing their depredations to the eaſtward, and retired to Etâwa.

The Rohilla country being thus entirely freed from the Mahrattas, Suja-al-Dowlah began to preſs Hafiz Rahmut upon the forty lacks, due by his engagement, of which he (the Vizier) had agreed to make over a moiety to the Engliſh (over and above the ſtipulated monthly ſubſidy) as a conſideration for their aſſiſtance; and he was ſupported in his requiſition by the Britiſh

Britiſh commander in chief, who having aſſiſted at the original negociation, and given the treaty the ſanction of his counter-ſignature, had a right to inſiſt on the punctual obſervance of it.—They could not, however, get any thing more from Hafiz than general profeſſions, and acnowledgments of the juſtice of the debt, with excuſes of the inability of the Rohillas to diſcharge it, or any part of it, at preſent, owing to the deſolated ſtate of their territories. The Vizier would willingly have taken occaſion, from hence, to appropriate the country of Hafiz Rahmut in lieu of the debt; a ſtep in which he would certainly have been fully juſtified by the Rohillas' treacherous breach of faith in this as well as in other particulars;—and he held forth ſome very advantageous offers about this time to the Britiſh government (through the commander in chief) for their aſſiſtance in the proſecution of a deſign he had formed to this purpoſe:—but as the Mahrattas were ſtill in great force in the *Doâb*, and might probably endeavour

vour to poſſeſs themſelves of the provinces of Korah and Allehabâd (which were the original objects of protection) whilſt Suja-al-Dowlah and his allies ſhould be engaged in this buſineſs, it was judged prudent to decline entering upon it; and it was thought at any rate moſt expedient, both in juſtice and in policy, * to give the Rohillas full time, that they might have a fair opportunity to fulfil their obligations before any meaſures ſhould be adopted to compel them.

In the mean time, as the ſeaſon was already very far advanced, and the country was reſtored to perfect tranquillity, the Britiſh and Vizier's troops returned into the province of Owde, and the former were ſtationed in cantonments at Sultanpore upon the Gûmty (a river which runs

* Perhaps a want of money and deficiency of political ſyſtem were more cogent reaſons than any other for relinquiſhing this undertaking at the preſent period.

through the province of Owde, washing Lucknow in its course) to serve as a check upon the future designs of the Mahrattas.

What farther views these marauders might have entertained is not positively known; but, happily for the peace of those provinces, which had for five years groaned under their wasteful depredations, the whole were about this period suddenly called off by the troubles at *Poona*, where Ragonet Row had put to death the Peishwá, his nephew, succeeded him in his office, and had been afterwards deposed by the faction of Sindhea and other chiefs; so that the affairs of their government were thrown into the utmost confusion, and their country threatened with a civil war; which rendered the presence of Toko Jee Holcar and his army absolutely necessary at Poona, in order to give a decided weight in favour of the new administration.—— They accordingly called in all their detachments, and withdrawing the whole of their forces from the Doâb, excepting a ſmall body which was ſtationed at Etâwa, went off to their own dominions, without leaving any eſtabliſhment to retain poſſeſſion or collect the revenues of the diſtricts they had lately overrun in the northern part of that territory.——Ahmed Khan Buxy (who had ſurrendered to Toko Jee Holcar at Ramghaut)* was at this period releaſed by the Mahratta commander, who preſented him with an elephant and palenkin, and diſmiſſed him with ſuch tokens of cordiality and reſpect as raiſed a ſuſpicion (perhaps not ill founded) of ſome colluſive management in the affair of Ramghaut, where the Buxy had exhibited ſuch a glaring deficiency in the proſecution of thoſe meaſures which were neceſſary for the repulſe of the enemy.

In fact, the characteriſtick treachery of the Rohillas, and their continually endeavouring to circumvent or overturn each other, was ruinous to the cauſe on every

* Page 186.

occaſion which required exertion and unanimity, and ſeemed to increaſe with the increaſe of their misfortunes, ſo as at once to excite the reſentment of their allies, and render them incapable of oppoſing its effects.—This ſpirit, ſo detrimental to their welfare, and ſo ruinous to them in its ultimate conſequences, appears in every anecdote reſpecting the internal adminiſtration of their government; and a moſt ſtriking inſtance of it was at this time manifeſted, in the treatment of Sydoola Khan's Begum, and of Mahummed-Yâr Khan, the fourth ſon of Allee Mahummed, and now, excepting Fyzoola-Khan, the only ſurvivor.——It has already been obſerved that the guardians, on making a final partition of the province of Kuttâher among themſelves, in detriment to thoſe who, although they poſſeſſed no *legal* title, were nevertheleſs, as the children of Allee Mahummed, the natural heirs to his uſurpations, had provided for the ſubſiſtence of Sydoola-Khan, by a penſion *, for the

* Page 121.

payment

payment of which funds were eſtabliſhed by each of the four principal chiefs granting aſſignments (to the amount ſpecified in the agreement) upon that portion of the territory which fell to his ſhare in the aforeſaid general partition.—Theſe aſſignments were made over to the Buxy, who was authorized, from the nature of his office, to collect the money and apply it to the intended purpoſe.

On the deceaſe of Sydoola Khan, a penſion of three lacks of rupees per annum was continued, in like manner, to the Begum his widow:—this, however, was very irregularly paid; and the late incurſions of the Mahrattas having deſolated Rohilcund in many places, furniſhed a pretext for withholding it altogether.—On the Mahrattas withdrawing into their own country, the Begum, ſhortly after the Buxy's releaſe, ſeized the opportunity of the chiefs being ſtill together in the field, to lay before them a repreſentation of her claims, and the diſtreſs under which ſhe

ſhe laboured, and intreated the diſcharge of the arrears due upon her penſion: at the ſame time Mahummed-Yâr Khan made loud complaints of the injurious and cruel neglect he ſuſtained, and of the miſery to which he was reduced from the total want of a maintenance.—Hafiz Rahmut, on their applying to him, with his uſual duplicity referred them to the *Buxy*, as the perſon who was reſponſible for the liquidation of all publick demands: the Buxy, however, denied in the ſtrongeſt terms his obligation to continue the payment of the Begum's penſion, unleſs he ſhould be enabled to do ſo by the ſeveral chiefs granting freſh aſſignments upon thoſe parts of their country which, not having ſuffered from the late invaſions, were now in a productive ſtate: the ſons and co-heirs of Doondy Khan, on being ſolicited in this behalf, at once rejected the appeal, declaring their father's agreement to contribute to the ſupport of Allee Mahummed's family in no wiſe binding upon them.—At length, after much fruitleſs negotiation,

negotiation, Hafiz, in order to put an end to the matter for the preſent, privately ſent a meſſage by a confidential ſervant to the Buxy, adviſing him to give written obligations to the Begum and to Mahummed-Yâr Khar, as well for the arrears due to the former, as for the payment of a regular annuity to the latter; adding——
"that when the Rohilla army ſhould be
"diſbanded, and the people ſeparated to
"their ſeveral places of abode, he could
"then, without danger of any popular
"inſurrection in favour of the parties,
"conſult his own convenience with re-
"ſpect to the fulfilment of them:"—This inſidious advice the Buxy ſtrictly conformed to, and prevailed upon Mahummed-Yâr and the Begum to accept thoſe frail teſtimonials of their rights; but never afterwards paid them a ſingle rupee; and even wreſted from the former a ſmall farm, producing about ſeven thouſand rupees per annum, which had been ſettled upon him by Buxy Sirdâr Khan.

Soon after the Mahrattas had evacuated Rohilcund, Futteh-Khan Khanſaman was ſeized with a palſy in his left ſide, of which he died in a few weeks.—He left ſix ſons, of whom the two eldeſt, Ahmed Khan and Azeem Khan, ſhared his territory between them, the diſtricts of Owlah and its dependances falling to the former, and thoſe of Budâvon and Owſte to the latter.—Scarcely were the ſons of Futteh Khan inſtated in their inheritance, when, according to the uſual mode of proceeding among the Rohillas, each endeavoured to ſubvert the other, and to eſtabliſh himſelf in ſole poſſeſſion of his father's lands and eſtates. In this Ahmed Khan, who was by much the abler politician, ſucceeded.—This feud between the brothers firſt broke out in conſequence of an effort, on the part of Azeem Khan, to retain in his own hands the whole of the elephants, artillery, and camp equipage, of his father, which were ſtationed at Owſte at the period of his deceaſe.—Upon this being compromiſed through the mediation of Hafiz Rahmut,

Rahmut, who compelled Azeem Khan to deliver up a moiety of the artillery and ſtores to Ahmed Khan, the latter affected to treat his brother with the utmoſt confidence and cordiality; and having by this means thrown him off his guard, ſuddenly marched to Owſte with a few reſolute followers, and there ſeizing on all the treaſures and effects which had been left in that place by the deceaſed, acquired, by this manœuvre, ſuch a decided ſuperiority, as conſtrained Azeem Khan to relinquiſh the whole of his inheritance, and to fly for ſafety to Peeleabete, where Hafiz Rahmut gave him protection, but could not, or would not, procure him any redreſs; and even acceded to Ahmed Khan ſucceeding his father in the office of Khânſaman.

The death of Futteh Khan left Hafiz Rahmut the only remaining perſon of theſe into whoſe hands Allee Mahummed had committed the management of the Rohilla government for his children, and in him the oſtenſible power of the ſtate now

 became

became veſted, as Fyzoola Khan and his brother had never been admitted to any efficient participation of it.—Hafiz Rahmut, notwithſtanding his very advanced age, ſtill perhaps poſſeſſed ſpirit and abilities ſufficient to have enabled him to bear with ſucceſs the great weight thus thrown upon his ſhoulders, had any tolerable degree of harmony ſubſiſted among the other leading members of the community; but that unanimity which alone could render them formidable now no longer prevailed among them; the authority of Hafiz, as "chief guardian of the ſtate," was ſlighted by ſome, and openly renounced by others; they regarded the ſuperiority he aſſumed with envy; and the manner of his attaining that pre-eminence had rendered him particularly obnoxious to the ſons of Allee Mahummed and their party; ſo that he found himſelf tottering on the pinnacle of an uſurped authority, without the ſupport of a ſingle friend in whom he could venture to confide.

In

In addition to a total defect in mutual alliance and general co-operation, many other circumſtances concurred to weaken the power of the Afgan independances in the northern provinces at this period.—Zabita Khan had been drawn off from their intereſt, as already related; and the death of Ahmed Khan Bungiſh left the principality of Ferrochabad in the hands of his ſon Muzziffer Jung, a weak and ignorant young man, who, ſo far from being able to add force or ſtability to any union which might have been entered into by them for their general defence, had it not in his power to ſupport himſelf; and was conſtrained, the year before, to have recourſe to Suja-al-Dowlah for his aid to protect his city from the attempts of a petty detachment of Mahrattas:—add to this, that in Rohilcund, the ſeeds of contention, which had been ſown in the original formation of the government, had long ſince ſprung up: a mutual jealouſy and avowed animoſity, which had effectually eſtranged the different leaders from each other, induced every

 man

man, in the present unsettled state of affairs, to aspire at a separate independence utterly inconsistent with their political consequence as a collective body; and the total relaxation or suspension of the penal laws, attendant upon such a state of anarchy, could not fail of producing the most mischievous effects, among a people naturally of a fierce and untoward temper, and possessed of a disposition so addicted to violence and rapine, as would at any time have required the severest exertions of justice to restrain it within bounds. The Hindoo farmers, and other *original* inhabitants of the country, groaned under the worst species of military vassalage; whilst the upstart Mussulman despots who held them in subjection, were, by their perpetual feuds, disabled, as we have seen, from affording them the smallest protection against armies of barbarous marauders, who every year spread their devastations among them, almost without resistance.—The haughty and turbulent spirit of the Afgans could not long submit to that strict con-

troul

troul which was neceſſary to preſerve any tolerable degree of regularity or ſubordination in a government compoſed of ſo many independent members:——conſequently orders were no longer heard or obeyed;—the adminiſtration of juſtice,—the collection of revenue,—and the intercourſe of commerce, were all at a ſtand;—the roads were infeſted with bands of armed ruffians; and every enormity had grown to ſuch a height as was not likely to yield to any remedy which, in the preſent ſtate of things, could poſſibly be applied.

Such was the ſtate of the Afgan powers in theſe countries a few months before the commencement of the celebrated "*Rohilla War.*"

Suja-al-Dowlah had, in his correſpondence with the Engliſh government, repeatedly expreſſed an earneſt deſire to have an interview with Mr. Haſtings, then governor of Bengal;—and many points of the utmost consequence having occurred in the course of his intimate connection with the British, the adjustment of which could not any way be so well effected as by a personal conference, the council at Calcutta were of opinion, that a meeting between their President and the Vizier at this season would be productive of great benefit to the affairs of the Company: Mr. Hastings was accordingly provided by them with especial powers of negotiation, and arrived at Benares in the month of August, A. D. 1773.

It may be recollected that Suja-al-Dowlah, at the close of the last campaign against the Mahrattas, in consequence of Hafiz Rahmut's apparent treachery, and breach of his engagements, had conceived an idea of seizing upon the Rohilla country, and had even made proposals to the British commander in chief for the assistance of the English troops in the immediate execution of this design. His proposals were, at that time, for many prudential and political reasons, rejected: these

theſe reaſons, however, *now* no longer exiſted:--the Mahrattas, whoſe preſence had formed the grand obſtacle to the undertaking, had gone off, and were now ſolely occupied in ſettling the internal diſſenſions of their own country; and many months had paſſed, within which the Rohillas, if ſo diſpoſed, could with eaſe have diſcharged the ſtipulated ſubſidy ſo juſtly due to the Vizier and his Allies, for having twice cleared their country of an enemy; but, inſtead of ſo doing, they had anſwered to the repeated importunities of the Vizier on this ſubject, by a reiteration of ſubterfuges, delays, and excuſes, which plainly indicated an intention on their part of never diſcharging the obligation.

In conſequence of this ſtate of things, the Vizier, in his conference with Mr. Haſtings at Benares, propoſed that the Britiſh government ſhould aſſiſt him with a brigade of the Company's forces, to enable him to effect the complete ſubjugation

tion of Rohilcund; and agreed to pay a monthly ſubſidy of two lacks and ten thouſand rupees, for the ſubſiſtence of theſe troops, and to preſent the Company with a gratuity of forty lacks of rupees, on the final performance of this ſervice; and the plan of the expedition was projected, and, with the ultimate approbation of the council in Calcutta, determined to be undertaken as ſoon as the ſeaſon fit for action ſhould commence, in the event of the Rohillas not diſcharging their obligations in the interim.—Almoſt immediately after, however, the Vizier, on a review of the neceſſary ſteps preparatory to this important undertaking, began to be apprehenſive that the period which he had fixed for its commencement, would ſcarcely allow him time to ſettle a variety of concerns, the previous adjuſtment of which was indiſpenſably requiſite to its ultimate ſucceſs, and which his eagerneſs for the attainment of his grand object had cauſed him to neglect or overlook at the time of his propoſing it; neither was he without

fears,

fears that, if he ſhould meet with any unexpected difficulty in the proſecution of thoſe preparatory meaſures, he might, by that circumſtance, be rendered incapable of fulfilling his agreement with reſpect to the promiſed ſubſidy, in addition to the many pecuniary obligations which he already lay under to the Company. He therefore ſuddenly reſcinded his propoſals reſpecting the ſubjugation of Rohilcund, expreſſing his wiſh that this matter ſhould (without being abſolutely relinquiſhed) remain in *ſuſpence*, the ultimate execution of it to depend upon the fortunate coincidence of future occurrences.

Soon after, Mr. Haſtings, having adjuſted the publick buſineſs with the Vizier, (the particulars of which are foreign to our ſubject) returned to Calcutta, and the Vizier to Fyzabad; from whence the latter proceeded without delay to the proſecution of thoſe meaſures by the ſucceſs of which his reſolution with reſpect to the Rohilcund

hilcund expedition was to be eventually determined.

His firſt object was the ſecurity of the diſtricts of Korah and Allehabad, and the eſtabliſhment of ſuch a line of defence on their northern frontier, from the Jumna to the Ganges, as would ſecure him in the undiſturbed poſſeſſion of them.—Theſe countries had been guaranteed to the impotent Emperor, Shah Aulum, by the treaty of Allehabad *, but were abandoned, and virtually relinquiſhed by him on his proceeding to Delhi †, where he ſhortly after made them over, by a grant, to the Mahrattas ‡, who would certainly have obtained a permanent ſettlement in them, which from their ſituation, muſt have been highly dangerous, if not utterly deſtructive, to the ſafety and independence of all the eaſtern provinces, had not their ſchemes been moſt fortunately fruſtrated by the timely and deciſive interference of

* Page 158.—† Page 170.—‡ Page 171.

the

the Engliſh ;—and they were confirmed to Suja-al-Dowlah in the late conference at Benares.

The Mahrattas, although they had been compelled, by the preſent deranged ſituation of their affairs at home, to relinquiſh a great part of their poſſeſſions in the *Doáb*, (as has been already obſerved) had yet left ſome ſmall garriſons in the diſtrict of Etâwa, which makes the northern boundary of the Korah province; and, as their eſtabliſhment here might enable them to give him great diſturbance at ſome future period, the Vizier judged it prudent to begin by ejecting them. He accordingly croſſed the Ganges at Mow, and marching over the *Doáb* *, laid ſeige to the fort of Etáwa.—The Mahratta who commanded in that fortreſs, after a ſmall reſiſtance, merely to ſave appearances, was prevailed upon to make a capitulation, by which the Mahrattas in this and other

* Oct. 1773.

places

places of the Doâb, were permitted to retire unmolested beyond the Jumna, and Suja-al-Dowlah had the good fortune to possess himself of the whole of these districts without any farther opposition; so that his dominion between the rivers now extended from Allehabad near to Agra upon the Jumna, and to Kinnoge upon the Ganges.

This great and unexpected success, by removing every obstacle of any moment, determined the Vizier to adhere to the execution of his original design; and he forthwith wrote to the Council at Calcutta, conveying formal proposals, in the terms already mentioned, which, after due deliberation, were acceded to, nearly on the same conditions as had been specified in the interview at Benares *.

The Rohilla expedition being now irrevocably determined on, as it was yet early in the season †, the Vizier resolved to

* Page 212.—† Dec. 1773.

smooth

ſmooth or remove every remaining obſtacle to his views, which, as his main object had been already attained with ſo much facility, he concluded he might eaſily effect, before his allies ſhould be in readineſs to take the field. Having taken proper precautions for the ſecurity of his own acquiſitions in the *Doâb*, by placing *Aumils* *, ſupported by conſiderable bodies of troops, throughout the country, he proceeded to Ferrochabad. Notice has already been taken of the wretched ſituation to which that ſtate had been reduced by the death of Ahmed Khan Bungiſh, and the imbecility of his ſucceſſor, whom Suja-al-Dowlah now eaſily found means to cajole with aſſurances of his friendſhip and ſupport, and finally to draw him into ſuch engagements as left his country, property, and perſon at the ſole diſpoſal of the Vizier, who ſoon found himſelf as entirely poſſeſſed of Ferrochabad as of any part of his own original dominions. From hence he ſent for Zabita Khan, who, having been releaſed from his

* Angice—" Superintendants, or collectors of revenue."

engagements

engagements with the Mahrattas, by their precipitate retreat from the *Doâb*, had retired to Nijeebabad, seeming inclined once more to join the fortunes of his countrymen;—but Suja-al-Dowlah, by his professions, not only detached him from their interests, but even persuaded him to join in the intended undertaking against them. —At the same time, the Vizier, apprehensive, perhaps, of some molestation from Nudjiff Khan, who had lately risen to a considerable degree of power, and, after the retreat of the Mahrattas, managed the Emperor's affairs at Delhi, endeavoured to secure his interest by making him privy to his design; and, it is said, even went so far as to hold forth some indirect promises of making over to his Majesty a share of whatever he should conquer; in consequence of which the minister entered with zeal into his designs, and agreed to join the Vizier with a select body of troops as soon as the campaign should commence.

Every thing being now ripe for action, Suja-

Suja-al-Dowlah direct his general, Litâfet Alee Khan, to march up the Ganges from Ferrochabad, and to construct a bridge of boats over the river at Ramghaut, by which he meant to enter at once into the heart of the Rohilla country; but whilst Litâfet was collecting materials for this purpose, the Vizier, by the advice of some English officers, abandoned that design, and determined to enter the Rohilla frontiers from his own dominions on the other side of the Ganges; as from thence the army would be able to draw the most certain and regular supplies, and the operations of the English forces were, by the terms of the treaty, confined to the *eastward* of that river. He accordingly returned to Mow, (where a bridge had been already laid) and crossing the river, advanced up the eastern bank, and encamped at Shawbad, on the Rohilla frontiers. From hence he deputed a Vakeel to Hafiz Rahmut, with a copy of his engagement*, and with orders to make

* App. No. I. and II.

a formal demand of immediate payment, on pain of the consequences.

In the mean time, the second brigade of the Company's forces took the field in the beginning of the year 1774, under the command of Colonel A. Champion, and advanced by easy marches to join the Vizier, according to agreement.

When Litâfet began to collect materials for constructing a bridge at Ramghaut, the Rohillas became sensible of the approaching storm;—their apprehensions were confirmed by the subsequent march of the English troops; and, on the receipt of the aforesaid message from the Vizier, Hafiz Rahmut amused the Vakeel with hopes of success in his deputation; and, in the mean time, applied to the several chiefs, desiring them either to enable him forthwith to discharge this demand, or to join him in the field:—they had already resolved on the latter alternative. The Vakeel, after some delay, was sent back to his master with an

evasive

evaſive anſwer, and Hafiz Rahmut proceeded from Peeleabete to Owlah, where he ſet up his ſtandard, and ſent notices throughout the country, requiring the Rohillas to repair thither.——Here he was ſoon joined by Fyzoola Khan and others; and as no remedy now appeared except open reſiſtance, Hafiz attempted to inſpire into the ſeveral leaders a reſolution to act with unanimity and firmneſs in ſupport of the common cauſe: but all his efforts were rendered void by that ſpirit of jealouſy and faction already mentioned, which contributed to deſtroy them much more effectually than the ſword of the enemy.

Hafiz firſt applied to Ahmed Khan Khanſaman, and Ahmed Khan Buxy, for money for the purpoſe of raiſing troops and making the neceſſary preparations; as theſe chiefs were, by their offices, inveſted with the management of all receipts and diſburſements that might at any time be neceſſary for the defence of the general ſtate.—He at the ſame time offered them

 bonds

bonds of indemnification, engaging either to hold himſelf perſonally reſponſible, or to give aſſignments upon his country for ſuch ſums as they might advance from their own finances for the public ſervice on the preſent occaſion. Notwithſtanding theſe aſſurances, however, they did not entertain ſuch an opinion of Hafiz as would induce them to place any dependance upon his promiſes, and having previouſly entered into a private league to ſupport each other, abſolutely refuſed to advance any money, declaring " they would " oppoſe with force whoever ſhould offer " to compel them." The Buxy, however, was perſuaded, by ſome of the more wiſe and diſcreet among his friends, to adopt a more liberal mode of conduct, at leaſt in *appearance*; and advanced two lacks of rupees for *tuncaws*, or aſſignments, upon the territory of Budâvon, which were given to him by the Khanſaman as a ſecurity;—" perhaps" (ſays the Rohilla narrator) " neither the perſuaſions of his " countrymen, nor his own conviction of " the

" the approaching danger, would have " ſufficed to induce the Buxy to this exer- " tion; but, from the period of the quar- " rel between the brothers" (Ahmed Khan and Azeem Khan) " he had regarded the " diſtrict of Budâvon with a greedy eye, " and an aſſignment, which would give " him a future hold upon it, offered ſuch " a temptation as he could not reſiſt." (Here we ſee, in the midſt of immediate apprehenſion and diſtreſs, and at a period of impending calamity, an involution of ſub-tile treachery, which is ſeldom outſhone in the crooked mazes of political refinement in uſe among the moſt *poliſhed* nations;— but to return—) Several other chiefs threw ſmall ſums into the grand treaſury upon the preſent exigency; but this mode of ſupply was not generally adopted, and af-ter all, the ſum collected was very inſuffi-cient to defray the neceſſary charges. In fact, ſo low were their finances reduced by their dominions for the two preceding years having been the ſeat of war, that few of the Rohilla chiefs had it in their power to contribute largely:—the only perſons among them whoſe circumſtances enabled them to do ſo were Hafiz Rahmut, the *Khanſaman*, (enriched by the plunder of his brother) and Fyzoola Khan, (who had long held the diſtricts of Rampore, from which, although not exceeding in value *five lacks* per annum, he had ſaved conſiderably, beſides what he acquired by ſucceeding to the inheritance of the perſonal property of his father)— and neither of theſe were willing to put too much to a riſk on the preſent occaſion.—Many other leading men, inſtead of coming boldly forward on this threatening emergency, ſeemed either abandoned to inactive deſpondency, or withheld from exertion by ſuſpicious doubts of their fellows, each conceiving the other to be ready to betray him; and Suja-al-Dowlah, well aware of their preſent temper, employed a multitude of emiſſaries among them, who, by working upon the hopes of ſome, and the fears of others, increaſed their mutual jealouſy and diſtruſt. Neither the Buxy nor the

the Khanſaman joined the Rohilla army till ſome time after its formation ; the Vizier having entered into a negotiation with them, and, partly by threats, partly by promiſes, prevailed on them (whatever appearance prudence might render neceſſary) to remain eſſentially *neuter* in the enſuing diſpute; and they were themſelves ſufficiently diſpoſed, in the preſent ſituation of things, rather to *forſake* than to *aſſiſt* their countrymen.; as they knew that if the Afgans ſhould make an effectual reſiſtance and repel the invaders, Hafiz would amply revenge himſelf upon them for their late oppoſition to him. Mahboola Khan and Fittee Oolah Khan (the ſons of Doondy Khan) neglected to appear in the field, or to aſſiſt in any meaſures of general co-operation until ſeveral days after the enemy had entered into the country, as they had alſo privately received a meſſage from Suja-al-Dowlah, who ſent them a *Koran*, (a ſacred pledge of mutual faith among Muſſulmans) with aſſurances of his protection, provided they ſhould not join Hafiz Rahmut on the present occasion; and to this they returned a favourable reply; but, with a fraudulent inconsistency, perfectly in character, they proceeded to Owlah at the head of a considerable force within four days after!

Perhaps, indeed, these intrigues of Suja-al-Dowlah (whose character was well known) would have availed but little in shaking the fidelity of any of the chiefs, had not they been strengthened in their operation by the general dread of Hafiz Rahmut.

To investigate the causes of this sentiment, which on the present occasion was attended with such fatal effects to the interest of the Rohilla confederacy in general, and of Hafiz Rahmut in particular, it is necessary to take a short retrospect to some incidents which could not have been related in their proper place without an unseasonable interruption to the narrative.

On the death of Futté Khan Khanſaman, Hafiz Rahmut took advantage of the quarrel between his heirs to ſeize on ſome of the lands and effects of that officer, and even refuſed to pay to his ſon and ſucceſſor Ahmed Khan an old debt of two lacks of rupees, which he had owed to the Khanſaman for ſome years paſt :——He had, moreover, exacted at another time the ſum of two lacks of rupees from the new Buxy, on pretence of defraying the expences of Allee Mahummed's youngeſt ſon, Mahummed-Yâr Khan, and applied the money ſo extorted to his own uſe ;—and, after the death of Doondee Khan, he had made frequent requiſitions of his ſons Mahboola and Fittee Oolah, under the ſame pretence.—In ſhort, from the time that the death of his colleagues had thrown the principal power into his own hands, Hafiz Rahmut had ſo often made an intemperate uſe of the oſtenſible authority with which, as " chief guardian of the ſtate," he was veſted, (and which he had been able to ſupport only by ſuperiority of military force

force and territorial refources) that, however refpected for his abilities and bravery, and revered for the apparent fanctity of his manners, he was almoft univerfally dreaded and difliked; and as he was aware of this difpofition in his countrymen, the intrigues he continually kept on foot, to fupport his influence, had confiderably widened the breaches before exifting among the members of a naturally turbulent and diftracted ftate:—even Fyzoola Khan, from whom alone he could expect effectual fupport, was not without fufpicions that Hafiz had at this period projected a plan to raife up a dangerous rival againft him in the perfon of his brother Mahummed-Yâr, and looked to the time when his own property might fall a facrifice to the crooked politicks and infatiable avarice of his wily guardian.—" To fum " up all," fays the Rohilla narrator, " a " fufprifing degree of animofity and dif- " cord had long fince arifen in Rohilcund, " and each perfon was employed in (nay, " was earneftly *bent upon)* the eradication " of

" of his neighbour ; and in order to effect " the destruction and overthrow of his " own immediate kindred and connec- " tions, was ready to enter into league " with foreigners and strangers : the event " was what might be expected, — what " indeed soon appeared in the course of " the succeeding occurrences."—In such circumstances, it is not surprising that, even at *this* awful moment, when a foreign enemy was about to overwhelm them, the chiefs were so dubious of each other that no general system of defence was adopted, nor any orders executed with the promptitude and alacrity necessary in so critical a juncture.

Such was the ruinous situation of affairs in the Rohilla camp, when the combined armies of Suja-al-Dowlah and his British allies entered their country on the 12th day of April, 1774 *.

On

* As the writer has been desirous (for very obvious reasons) to adhere closely to the account given by

On the allied army crossing the river Gûrra, (which intersects the southern boundary of Rohilcund near Shawbad) several Zimeendars, and some governors of districts upon the borders, came in to the Vizier and threw themselves upon his mercy; and were permitted to remain unmolested in their habitations: but, as it was judged imprudent to leave any shelter to those, who by their behaviour appeared to be inimicably inclined, and who, as the army advanced, might, by returning to their habitations, be the means of interrupting the free communication with the Vizier's country, and cutting off the supplies, his troops burned and destroyed the villages of such as had refused to submit, or had abandoned them on his approach.

Fyzoola

by the *Rohil'a*, in his relation of the subsequent transactions, he hopes that this motive will be considered as a sufficient apology for any inaccuracies that may appear in it; he has blended the *English* account with it, as far as is consistent with his adherence to the other.

Fyzoola Khan now became ſo ſenſible of the inability of the Rohilla forces to reſiſt the power which was brought againſt them, that he repeatedly applied to Hafiz Rahmut, intreating him, if poſſible, to come to an accommodation with the Vizier, and offering himſelf to undertake the payment of his demands, by exerting his intereſt with the other chiefs, and perſuading them to contribute to the diſcharge of them;—but Hafiz, with a wilful perverſeneſs which ſeemed to urge him to his fate, declined accepting of any of thoſe overtures, and determined, at all events, to try his fortune in the field.

On the 17th of April, Hafiz, who aſſumed the chief command of the Rohilla army, marched with his whole force, conſiſting of about twenty-four thouſand horſe and foot, four thouſand rocket men, and ſixty pieces of cannon and amuzettes, and the next day took poſt near the village of Cutterah, on the banks of the *Bogga*, his

his rear and one of his flanks being covered by that river.

Colonel Champion, who was commander in chief of the Britiſh and Vizier's forces, advanced on the 20th to Shahjehanpôre, and on the two ſucceeding days made ſome feints, as if he intended to take a circuit and advance into the interior part of the country, without coming to action; the apprehenſion of which would conſtrain the Rohillas to relinquiſh the advantages of the judicious poſition they had choſen.

Hafiz Rahmut, who had for two days expected to ſee the enemy, and kept his troops under arms for ſeveral hours each morning to be in readineſs for their reception, conſiderably relaxed his vigilance when he found that, inſtead of coming directly upon him, they were employed in meaſures which indicated an intention of turning his rear, and thereby cutting off his communication with Owlah and

Barêllee.

Barêllee, from whence alone the Rohillas could draw the ſupplies neceſſary to their ſubſiſtence. Alarmed at this idea, he made ſome change in his poſition, with an intention of retreating to the laſt of theſe towns, ſhould circumſtances render this meaſure neceſſary.

On the 22d, the Britiſh commander, finding that his manœuvres had produced their intended effect, made the neceſſary preparation for action, and marching the next morning at two o'clock, without beat of drum, threw his baggage and followers into a ſmall fort which had been deſerted by the enemy, and came within view of the Rohilla camp a little after ſun-riſe.

Nothing could exceed the aſtoniſhment of Hafiz Rahmut, when he underſtood that the whole army of the enemy were drawn up in battle array, within cannon ſhot of his encampment, after having beat in the out-poſted guards, who were the firſt meſſengers of the alarm. He directly mounted his elephant in order to go forth and reconnoitre their position, whilst in the mean time the Rohillas were thrown into a general confusion by the near and unexpected approach of their adversaries.—— Hafiz Rahmut, when he rode out, had neglected to order the *Nekkâreh* (or alarm drum) to beat, so that a considerable time elapsed before any line was formed, or the artillery prepared for action, and no general plan of operations having been settled, nor any orders received, every leader acted as he thought proper.—About four thousand of their infantry, seeing things in such disorder, retired, panick struck, from the field; and when Hafiz returned to the camp, he found a great part of the troops ready to follow their example; his presence, however, restored them to some degree of order, and inspired them with a resolution to make one brave effort for the preservation of their independence.

Hafiz took his post in the centre of the Afgan army, which was directly opposed to to the Britiſh troops :—Fyzoola and Muſtakeem Khan, with ſome of the other principal chiefs, led on that diviſion of their forces oppoſite to the corps of Litâfet and the Vizier's ſepoys ; and they were at this inſtant joined by Mahboola Khan and his brother Fittee Oolah, who had left Biſſeeolee with their followers the preceding day.

The action conſiſted principally of a cannonade, which was ſupported above two hours with great ſpirit on both ſides, at firſt at the diſtance of a thouſand yards, which, as the armies gradually advanced towards each other, was afterwards reduced to five hundred : the powder of the Rohillas being of a very bad quality, moſt of their ſhot fell ſhort ; and their rockets, although thrown in prodigious quantities, did but little execution ; whilſt a continual ſhower of balls fell upon their centre from the Engliſh artillery, and made dreadful havock in their unwieldy columns.—Many attempts were made by

Muſtakeem Khan and others to lead the cavalry to the charge, and to force the enemy's flanks, but without effect.—At length, Hafiz, ſeeing the ſpirit of the ſoldiers begin to droop under the ſuperior fire of the Engliſh, deſcended from the elephant which he had hitherto rode, and mounted an ordinary horſe, to convince his followers that he had no intention of eſcaping, but was determined to conquer or die.—Very ſoon after this, he, on whom every thing depended, fell. — The center ſeeing the fate of their general, immediately began to give way; and in a few minutes the whole broke, and fled with precipitation, leaving their camp (which was ſtill ſtanding) with all their baggage and artillery to the victors.

Immediately on the Rohillas giving way, ſome bodies of the Vizier's cavalry were detached in purſuit; and the flying troops, in order to ſave themſelves from total deſtruction, all ſeparated, and went off to different

different places, ſo that in a few hours the Rohilla army no longer exiſted.

The loſs ſuſtained by the Vizier and his Allies in this deciſive action was inconſiderable; but that of the Afgans was not leſs than two thouſand killed and wounded; and their whole ſyſtem ſuffered an irreparable blow in the death of their gallant leader.

Thus fell Hafiz. Râhmut, who (notwithſtanding his low original) whether we conſider him as a ſoldier or a ſtateſman, was certainly entitled to ſome degree of reſpect.—As the director of a factious and diſtracted government, he by the ſuperiority of his talents and addreſs kept together its ſeveral parts much longer, certainly, than could have been expected, conſidering the nature of the people with whom he had to deal, and the unfortunate events under which they laboured.—His perſonal bravery and firmneſs in the hour of danger would have enabled the

Rohillas to ſupport themſelves with ſucceſs againſt all their foreign enemies, and to have protected their dominion from the many calamities in which it had been involved for ſome years paſt, had he been properly ſupported by his colleagues; and it was this ſpirit that determined him, on the failure of every other reſource, to prefer an honourable death to an inglorious ſubmiſſion. — But, however praiſeworthy his conduct in theſe ſituations may appear, the circumſtances of his riſe to power, as well as the uſe he often made of that power when acquired, —— muſt detract greatly from his merit!—and it remains to be regretted that ſuch happy endowments ſhould have been blended with the moſt miſchievous of all vices, and that a graſping and unprincipled ambition ſhould have induced him to betray the truſt of his friend, and uſurp the inheritance of his wards, in a manner which tarniſhes all his great qualities and throws a perpetual ſlur on his memory; nor was the fate he met with leſs *deſerved* than it has been,

been, by numbers, pitied and lamented *: but, to return.—

Fyzoola Khan and his brother Mahummed-Yâr, who had both exerted them-

* It is here neceſſary to remark that, (among a multitude of ſimilar errors) this perſon has been confounded with *Hafiz*, the famous poet of *Shirâz*, who flouriſhed above four hundred years ago.—It is much to be lamented that the warmth and eagerneſs of political reſentments, (however laudable their motives) ſhould ſometimes ſtimulate the moſt eminent characters, by haſtily adopting all circumſtances which can tend to aggravate imputed guilt, and putting them together without a ſufficient inquiry into the foundation of them, to ſully the pure and ſimple beauty of *Truth*, which needs not the turgid inflation of unfounded rhapſody to ſupport it:—" Hafiz Rahmut, the moſt " eminent of their chiefs,—*as famous throughout the* " *eaſt for the elegance of his literature and the ſpirit of* " *his poetical compoſitions (by which he ſupported the name* " *of Hafiz)* as for his courage, was invaded *," &c. &c.——Hafiz was neither a *poet* nor a man of letters. —His original name was *Rahmut Khan*:—The title of *Hafiz* (anglicé, the *protector*) he afterwards aſſumed, as being expreſſive of his rank and office.

* Parliamentary Regiſter, No. LXXVI. page 205.

ſelves with much gallantry in the foregoing action, when they heard that Hafiz was killed, uſed every effort to keep their troops together.—Fyzoola had attempted to make a charge upon Litâfet's corps; in this, however, he failed; and the Afgans ſaw the Britiſh line advancing upon them in ſuch excellent order that, dreading the effects of their muſquetry, neither the upbraidings nor intreaties of their leaders could induce them to ſtand; and they rode off the field at full gallop, hurrying *them* along with them.—Fyzoola Khan, ſeeing the army totally diſperſed, fled in deſpair to Rampore; and taking from thence his family and valuable effects, retired, by the route of Patterghûrr, to the ſtrong paſs in the Cummôw hills above Lolldông, which had twice before ſerved as a place of refuge to his countrymen; and here he was daily joined by numbers who preferred the deſperate chance of this laſt reſource to ſubmiſſion to the enemy on any terms.

Nothing could exceed the terror and confuſion

confufion of the Afgans throughout Rohilcund, on learning the difaftrous iffue of a battle which at once annihilated their power and decided the fate of their dominion ; and the news was quickly fpread abroad with all the exaggerations which commonly accompany the relation of any general and unexpected calamity.—Neither were their fears confined to the progrefs of the victorious army. Wherever the defeat of the Rohillas became known, the Hindoo Zimeendars (each of whom is poffeffed of a ftrong hold attaching to the chief village of his diftrict) fhut their forts, and refufing their late mafters fuccour or protection, plundered, without diftinction, all whom they found flying towards the hills; fo that numbers of the Afgans, who would otherwife have joined their countrymen at Lolldông, returned to their homes, and there quietly waited the event. —Many more, indeed, were encouraged to this by the generous and temperate conduct of the Britifh troops, whofe characteriftick virtues were not more difplayed by their gallantry in the late engagement, than by their humanity after it.——In the cloſe of the action, whilſt yet fluſhed with recent victory, they advanced by diviſions, and marched through the Rohilla camp with all the diſciplined coolneſs and regularity of a review; not a man offering to leave his poſt, or to ſeize on any part of the ſpoil which was ſcattered over the plain around them: and on the ſame evening all the wounded Rohillas who appeared to be in a curable ſtate were taken into the Engliſh hoſpital, and attended with the ſame care as their own people; and theſe circumſtances undoubtedly contributed not only to the reputation of the conquerors, but to the facility of their ſubſequent ſucceſs.

On the final flight of the Afgans, Mahummed-Yâr Khan, attended by the Buxy and the Khanſaman, went off to Owlah, where they arrived the ſame afternoon, and ſpent the night in all the confuſion of diſtracted councils and unavailing lamentations.

tions. In the morning, the two miniſters having collected together their families and treaſures, proceeded to the hills by the way of Biſſoolee and Moradabâd, and joined Fyzoola Khan, (who, on the death of Hafiz aſſumed the chief command) at Lolldông. Mahummed-Yâr Khan accompanied the miniſters to Biſſoolee, and from thence went with a few attendants through Sumbull to Fyrozabâd, where he found Mahummed Allee Khan, a perſon of influence and experience, and an old retainer of his father's. To him he declared his intentions of proceeding to Lolldông to join his brother, but was diſſuaded from this deſign by the arguments of Mahummed Allee, who aſſured him "that he "could not poſſibly paſs through the "country in ſafety, as the Zimeendars "were all up in arms:—that, as the family of Doondee Khan ſtill remained "at Biſſoolee, and thoſe of Hafiz Rahmut "with all their effects, at Peeleabete, he, "who poſſeſſed *nothing*, might ſurely retire to his own habitation without ap-"prehenſion

"prehension of danger, and thereby avoid "exposing his family to almost inevitable "destruction from the intense heats of the "present season; and the late conduct of "the English evinced that he had more to "hope from their kindness than to fear "from their resentment."——In conformity to this advice, Mahummed-Yâr Khan retired to his own place of residence at Owlah.

Mahboola Khan, and his brother Fittee Oolah, depending much upon the assurances which they had received from the Vizier previous to the battle of Cutterah, (although they had forfeited all title to this dependance by joining their friends in the engagement) retired to Bissoolee, their own city, and there remained.

The Begum widow of Sydoola Khan, (who resided at Owlah) on learning the death of Hafiz Rahmut, and the defeat of the Rohilla forces, immediately dispatched a messenger to Suja-al-Dowlah, "requesting

" ing to know his pleaſure with reſpect to
" her, whether he meant that ſhe ſhould
" ſurrender up her effects, or rely upon
" his generoſity".——In reply to this the Vizier immediately ordered two of his confidential ſervants to wait upon the Begum—" to aſſure her of his favourable in-
" tentions towards her, and to requeſt her
" not for a moment to admit any doubt or
" apprehenſion into her mind, nor by ill-
" grounded fears to diſſeminate confuſion
" and terror in the city of Owlah :—that
" her annual allowance, which, under the
" Rohilla chiefs, had never exceeded fifty
" thouſand rupees per annum, ſhould be
" increaſed to ſomething more proportion-
" able to her rank and ſituation ; and that
" ſhe might hope for every thing from his
" future kindneſs." Confiding in theſe declarations, the Begum remained at Owlah, and thereby preſerved the tranquillity of the city, where there was no more appearance of diſturbance or diſorder than if nothing extraordinary had happened.

The

The family of Hafiz Rahmut, with a torpid apathy which is not eafy to be accounted for, took no meafures either for flight or defence, but continued quietly in the fort of Peeleabête, apparently little moved by the late (to them) dreadful cataftrophe. Zoo-al-Fukkâr Khan, Hafiz's eldeft fon, who had fled to Barélle immediately after the battle, when he heard of Mahummed-Yâr Khan being at Owlah, went and joined him at that place.

Such were the immediate effects of the battle of Cutterah among the Rohillas: let us now return to the Vizier and his allies.

A body of Suja-al-Dowlah's horfe took poffeffion of the city of Barélle the night after the action. The victors enamped on the 23d, and the fucceeding day near the field of battle, and, on the 25th, leaving Barélle on their left, marched towards Peeleabête.——The family of Hafiz Rahmut, on hearing of the Vizier's approach, were rather pleafed than alarmed at the intelligence,

telligence, as their greateſt dread aroſe from the apprehenſion of ſome of the Rohillas taking this opportunity to retaliate upon them the former exactions of their deceaſed chief; againſt which they hoped, under the ſhelter of the Engliſh or the Vizier, to find a permanent protection.——"In ſhort," (ſays the narrator) "misfortune and infatuation was "their lot, in that they did not think "of taking refuge in the intrenchments at "the foot of the hills, which were at ſo "inconſiderable a diſtance, and where, "under the guardianſhip of Fyzoola "Khan, their honour and their property "would have remained ſecure and untouched, and they would have experi"enced every kind of attention and re"gard from that benignity for which he "is ſo juſtly famed." The event, indeed, ſoon evinced the folly of their inactivity.—The garriſon had already abandoned the place; ſo that, upon the allied troops appearing before it, it was ſurrendered without any reſiſtance; and the family of Hafiz

Rahmut

Rahmut, together with such treasure, jewels, &c. as remained from the wreck of his fortune, fell into the hands of the Vizier without stipulation or condition; and the next day all the women and children of the Haram were put into pelanquins and other covered carriages, and sent off under a strong guard to Owlah, whither the Vizier accompanied them.

Two days after the surrender of Peeleabête, the English troops fell back to Barél-lee, where they remained for some time, the commander in chief meaning to canton there during the ensuing rainy season; however, at the request of the Vizier, they removed from hence, and marched to Bissoolee. At this place they found Nudjiff Khan, who, in pursuance of his promise, had brought along with him a body of six thousand men to assist in the reduction of the Rohillas, but arrived too late to have any share in the foregoing service.

The two brothers, Mahboola Khan and

Fittee Oolah, when they beheld the fate of Hafiz Rahmut's family, began to entertain ſome doubts of the Vizier's intentions with reſpect to themſelves, eſpecially as they were conſcious that by their breach of a private agreement previouſly underſtood, (in joining Hafiz Rahmut in the battle, notwithſtanding their acceptance of the overtures from the Vizier) they muſt in ſome meaſure be conſidered as having forfeited that protecttion to which they might otherwiſe have laid claim :——they therefore now reſolved to *divide the hazard*, by one of the brothers proceeding to pay his reſpects to the Nabob, whilſt the other ſhould remain at Biſſoolee (where their families and treaſures were depoſited) and act as circumſtances might direct.—Accordingly, Fittee Oolah Khan proceeded to the Vizier's camp at Baréllee, and there, before he would venture to appear, ſolicited the mediation of Salar Jung (the Vizier's uncle) in his favour.—Some of his friends endeavoured to diſſuade the Rohilla from taking this ſtep, and adviſed him rather to apply to the Bri-

tiſh

tiſh commander "as it was well known "that when the Engliſh word was "pledged it could be relied on; whereas, "no faith could be placed either in the "Vizier himſelf or in any of his officers." Fittee Oolah, however, rejected this ſalutary council; and procuring an introduction to the Vizier the next day, immediately after being diſmiſſed from audience he was ordered into confinement.—In the interim, Mahboola Khan waited at Biſſoolee, under much anxiety to hear of his brother's ſucceſs, and would have availed himſelf of the intelligence he received concerning his reception, by removing with the moſt valuable part of his treaſure to join his countrymen at Lolldông; but his intention was at once fruſtrated by the unexpected appearance of Nudjiff Khan, who arrived at Biſſoolee the ſame evening, and either gueſſing the Rohilla's deſign, or being furniſhed with previous inſtructions, placed guards around his houſe, ſo that all hope of eſcape was extinguiſhed; and thus both the brothers experienced the natural

effects

effects of their indecisive and *trimming* policy.——Had they boldly rejected the Vizier's insidious offers in the first instance, and openly and gallantly shared the fortunes of their countrymen in their last retreat, their honour would still have remained untouched, and their persons free; but, by acceding to the Vizier's offers, and afterwards appearing against him in battle, they entailed upon themselves universal odium, and at the same time incurred his implacable resentment.

The day before the arrival of the allied army at Bissoolee, Mahummed-Yâr Khan came in, and being presented to the Vizier by his servants Mirza Ramzânee and Mirza Agâ, was very favourably received; nor did he ever afterwards suffer any molestation either in his person or family. Numbers of the other Rohillas, who had not accompanied their countrymen in their flight, on hearing this, came in, and found a similar reception.

From Owlah the Vizier wrote circular letters to all the remaining Afgans of any note throughout the country, desiring them to continue quietly in their dwellings, and giving them the most solemn assurances of protection. These delarations were in general attended with their full effect; in a few weeks all the country south of Rampore was put entirely into the possession of the Vizier, and every thing was soon reduced to perfect tranquillity.

Shortly after his arrival at Bissoolee, the Vizier sent off the sons of Doondee Khan, their wives and children, together with the family and immediate retainers of Hafiz Rahmut, and numbers of the Afgan inhabitants of Baréllee, Owlah, Bissoolee, and other places, to Allehabâd, under the conduct of his brother-in-law, the Nabob Salar Jung*.

On

* Much has been said of the *excessive cruelties* practised by Suja-al-Dowlah on his Rohilla prisoners, and in

On the commencement of the rainy ſeaſon, Suja-al-Dowlah and his allies built temporary quarters of cantonment in the neighbourhood of Biſſoolee, where a Hindoo named Beâſs Râye (who had been the Dewân of Hafiz Rahmut) inſinuated himſelf into the Vizier's favour, by giving him information reſpecting the ſecret depoſits of treaſure, &c. among the Rohillas, and being himſelf forward in committing acts of oppreſſion upon them.—To this man Suja-al-Dowlah rented the conquered country, at the rate of *two krores of rupees per annum*; but he was ſoon after diſplaced on account of his malverſations; the whole body of the people making loud

---

in particular, on the family of Hafiz Rahmut; the above, however, is *all* that is mentioned by the Rohilla narrator upon this ſubject; and, notwithſtanding every poſſible inquiry, the writer has never been able to diſcover a ſingle document from which he might aſcertain any one particular of this alledged ill uſage, unleſs the inconveniences neceſſarily attendant upon *confinement* and *removal* are to be termed ſuch.

complaints of the sufferings to which they were subjected under his administration.

Fyzoola Khan, on flying to the hills, perceiving the ruinous state of the Afgan cause, resolved to attempt every expedient to screen himself from that destruction in which the fortunes of so many of his countrymen were already involved; and hoped to obtain, by negotiation, a happier and more honourable settlement than the present situation of affairs afforded him any prospect of procuring by other means. Many circumstances, indeed, were in his favour.—As the eldest remaining son of Allee Mahummed, he was the ostensible heir to his possessions, however surreptitiously these possessions were obtained: the injustice done him by his guardians, his innocence with respect to the origin of the war, and his amiable character and manners (independant of other circumstances) all contributed to plead strongly in his behalf. —He therefore wrote to the commander in chief

chief of the Britiſh forces at Biſſoolee, propoſing, through the mediation of the Engliſh, to come to terms with the Vizier; and, on the 19th of May he deputed an Afgan named Abdureen Khan, to negotiate with Colonel Champion.—The Vakeel had inſtructions to propoſe *three* ſeveral modes of adjuſtment. The moſt feazible of theſe was, "that his maſter ſhould hold the whole of "*Kuttâher* in fealty of the Vizier, paying "him an annual tribute of forty lacks of "rupees,—the Britiſh government to re-"ceive from him a donation of thirty lacks "(on the part of the Company) as a re-"compence for their good offices in influ-"encing the Vizier to accede to theſe "terms."—The commander in chief wrote to the Council at Calcutta, ſtrongly recommending the propriety of their procuring this or ſome ſimilar compromiſe in behalf of the Rohilla chief: the Council, however, declined any interference between the principals in the war, under an apprehenſion (probably not ill-founded) that the Vizier might be led to explain ſuch an interposition into a breach of their treaty with him, which would afford him a pretext for not fulfilling his part of it; and they moreover objected to the proposed measure on grounds of political expediency *.

This

* The substance of the arguments used as reasons for the British government declining to interfere between the Vizier and Fyzoola Khan on this occasion is contained in the following extract of a letter written by Mr. Hastings, in answer to the representations of the commander in chief concerning it.

" WE engaged to assist the Vizier in reducing the " Rohilla country under his dominion, that the boun- " dary of his possessions might be completed by the " Ganges forming a barrier to cover them from the " attacks and insults to which they were exposed, by " his enemies either possessing, or having access to, " the Rohilla country: this our alliance with him, " and the necessity of maintaining this alliance so long " as he and his successors shall deserve our protection, " rendered advantageous to the Company's interest; " because the security of his possessions from invasions " in that quarter is, in effect, the security of our's: " but if the Rohilla country is delivered to Fyzoola " Khan, the advantages proposed from this measure " will

This negotiation neceſſarily occupied ſome time. Fyzoola Khan, however, did not in the interim neglect any meaſures which might be requiſite to enable him to make a vigorous defence in the laſt reſort. On his arrival at Lolldông, he had iſſued proclamations, inviting all the Afgans to join his ſtandard there.—During the interval of ſuſpenſion of hoſtilities, every means had been uſed by intrenchments and barricadoes to render the poſt at this place as tenable as poſſible; and multitudes of Rohillas, who would never otherwiſe have

" will be totally defeated. The ſame objections from " the *Vizier* will take place againſt him as againſt Hafiz Rahmut:—he will be actuated by the ſame principles of ſelf-defence, and the ſame impreſſions of " fear, to ſeek the protection of other powers againſt " the Vizier, and of courſe, will create the ſame jealouſies and ſuſpicions in the mind of the Vizier, " with the additional and ſtrong incentive of a mutual " animoſity, and of an enormous debt, which, probably, Fyzoola Khan will find no means to get " clear of, but by engaging in hoſtilities againſt the " Vizier."

thought of moving, were driven, by the exactions of the renter and his agents, to seek an asylum here; insomuch that, before the rains were yet fully set in, such intelligence was received of the situation and daily augmenting strength of the Afgans, as made it necessary, notwithstanding the severity of the season, to proceed against them without loss of time. There were, moreover, other cogent reasons for pushing the operations to a final conclusion at this period.—It was reported that the Vizier had entered into an agreement with the Emperor Shah Aulum, before the commencement of the Rohilla war, engaging to make over to his Majesty a moiety of whatever territory he should acquire either in the *Doâb* or in Rohilcund; in consideration of which agreement he had received, as *Vizier of the Empire*, a royal *firman*, "authorizing him to re-"duce the Afgan rebels in Rohilcund to obe-"dience:" and he was now honoured with a letter from the Emperor, "congratulating "him in the warmest terms on his late suc-

"cess,

" ceſs, and hinting at *the expected fulfilment* " *of his engagements.*" Theſe expectations on the part of the Emperor, whatever their foundation might be, would have given the Vizier little concern; but advices were at this time received that the Mahrattas had ſettled their political diſputes (all their internal commotions having ſubſided in conſequence of the expulſion of Ragonet Row) and were again ready to carry their arms to the northward. This left ſufficient room to foreſee that the Emperor might renew his connections with them; and as Suja-al-Dowlah, whether the alledged compact had ever been really executed or not, was now determined againſt acceding to his demands, it was to be apprehended that he would make uſe of the Mahrattas to enforce them; and the Vizier was aware that if he delayed proceeding againſt the remaining part of the Rohilla forces until the dry weather, as the Ganges, on the falling of the waters, became fordable in many parts below the poſt then occupied by the Afgans, he muſt,

by

by advancing, have left theſe paſſages conſiderably in his rear, which would have given his enemies opportunities to make incurſions, and lay waſte his dominions during his abſence on ſo remote a ſervice.—These conſiderations made the Vizier exceedingly anxious to bring the ſubjugation of Rohilcund to a ſpeedy and deciſive iſſue.—Accordingly, at his repeated ſolicitation and intreaty, the army again took the field, evacuating their cantonments at Biſſoolee on the 30th day of July, about the middle of the rainy ſeaſon.

There were, on the route to Lolldông, many poſts, the defence of which by the Rohillas, might have greatly retarded the progreſs of the allied troops at ſuch a ſeaſon; but they were ſo much diſpirited by the total defeat they had ſuſtained in the field, and ſuch diſtractions prevailed in their councils after that event, that none of them had attempted to occupy any of theſe favourable ſituations, but, abandoning the plain country altogether, had retired to their

their intrenchments in the hills; the army, therefore, proceeded entirely unmoleſted, and took poſſeſſion of the town of Nijeebabâd, and the fort of Pattergûrr, (ſituated about twenty miles from Lolldông) without reſiſtance.—The army encamped for ſome days in the neighbourhood of this place; and a negotiation was here opened between the Vizier and Fyzoola Khan, but without any effect; the Rohilla chief demanding ſuch terms of capitulation as were regarded by the Vizier to be very extravagant and inadmiſſible, conſidering the ſtate to which he was reduced.—On the 28th of Auguſt the allied army made a forward movement to Mohunpôre, a village near Byceghaut on the Ganges, which brought them within leſs than fifteen miles from the enemy; and from hence was formed a chain of poſts, ſo diſtributed as totally to intercept any ſupplies of proviſions from being carried into the Rohilla intrenchments. This meaſure decided the fate which had been ſo long impending, and was now about to overthrow the laſt remains of the Rohilla power.

power. The ſupplies which the Afgans drew from the hills in their rear were far from being ſufficient for their ſupport, as their number amounted to upwards of forty thouſand; and to add to their diſtreſs, a peſtilential diſorder (owing to the want of room and the unhealthineſs of their ſituation) broke out among them, and carried off many every day. But, notwithſtanding the diſtreſs in which they were involved, Fyzoola Khan ſtill continued to hold out with determined firmneſs and reſolution (ſuch as could have been little expected from the general tenor of his character) hoping, by his perſeverance, ſo far to delay the iſſue of the war, that ſome favourable circumſtances might fall out in the interim, which would conſtrain the Vizier to come to an accommodation upon terms more honourable than thoſe of abſolute and unconditional ſubmiſſion. Near a month was ſpent in treating on a variety of propoſitions advanced by the Rohilla Vakeels as the baſis of a treaty of adjuſtment. The general ſcope of theſe was, that Fyzoola Khan ſhould

ſhould pay the Vizier a large ſum in hand, and rent of him either the *whole* or a *part* of Rohilcund, at a proportionable rate, taking upon himſelf the diſburſement of all expences. The Vizier, however, conceived that theſe offers were by no means adequate to the magnitude of the object; and, moreover, many reaſons of ſound policy occurred to prevent his ſuffering the Afgans to re-eſtabliſh themſelves with any conſiderable degree of ſtrength in that country, a circumſtance which would, in fact, have been utterly ſubverſive of one of the leading principles upon which the war had been undertaken.—Yet, as he was extremely deſirous to come to a ſpeedy concluſion, he propoſed to grant to Fyzoola Khan a jagheer of fifteen lacks a year in the Doâb, on condition of his delivering up one half of his treaſure and effects.—This offer was certainly very equitable, and would have ſecured the Rohilla chief in much more than he had ever before poſſeſſed:—he was adviſed, however, by the Buxy and the Khanſaman, to reject this advantageous propoſal,

proposal; upon which it was judged necessary to take such measures as would reduce him to a more speedy determination; and accordingly, the main body of the Vizier's and English troops advanced from Mohunpôre, and penetrating through the woods, took post at the foot of the Cummôw hills, within two miles of the Afgan intrenchments, throwing up some redoubts and other works, (in sight of the advanced post of the Rohillas) such as indicated an intention of assaulting them in their lines. Still, however, the Rohillas continued to hold out with an obstinacy that seemed to increase in proportion to the misery which overwhelmed them.—The Buxy and Khansaman, and some other chiefs, who were particularly apprehensive of having offended the Vizier by the duplicity of their conduct, were resolved, at all hazards, not to yield, except on such terms as might secure them against the effects of his resentment; whilst he, on the other hand, irritated at what he interpreted into a contumacious rejection of his proffered grace,

now

now determined to compel them to ſurrender themſelves and their effects to his ſole uncontrollable diſpoſal.

But, whatever obſtructions the apprehenſions or animoſities of the belligerent parties might throw in the way of an amicable adjuſtment, things were now coming to a criſis—The Rohillas were reduced to the utmoſt diſtreſs; ſo that they could not poſſibly hold out many days longer; and muſt either have run the deſperate chance of throwing themſelves upon the Vizier's mercy, or endeavoured to make their eſcape over the hills by the paſſes and defiles which lead into the territories of *Sirnagûr* and *Kummâoon.* The Vizier was not without apprehenſions of their making ſuch an attempt, which, however deſtructive it might be to them, would at any rate deprive him of his expected ſpoil; and, in order to prevent it, he entertained ſome idea of ſtorming their intrenchments, a meaſure, which in the preſent weak ſtate of the Afgans, muſt have been attended with

with immediate ſucceſs. Happily, the prudence of Fyzoola Khan, and the reliance he placed upon the mediating protection of the Engliſh, led him, at length, to preclude the neceſſity of ſuch a ſanguinary ſtep. No more than four days proviſions now remained in his camp; even the horſes and camels had been all conſumed; —the nature of the country in his rear, interſected by deep ravines, and covered with impenetrable foreſts, rendered a retreat impracticable, or, at leaſt, likely to be attended with circumſtances more fatally deſtructive than even the ſword of the enemy; and he conceived that he had ſtill a reſource in the friendly interpoſition of the Britiſh commander in chief.—He therefore ſent a meſſage to Colonel Champion, teſtifying his deſire to come to him, in order that he might perſonally, through his means, effect an honourable accommodation with the Vizier.—Upon the receipt of this meſſage, two Engliſh officers were deputed to conduct the Rohilla chief into the Britiſh camp, whither he accompanied them

on

on the ſecond day of October; and, on the ſeventh of the ſame month, the treaties of peace were agreed upon and finally concluded *.

By this agreement, Fyzoola Khan had guarranteed to him the poſſeſſion of the diſtricts of Rampore and its dependencies, yielding an annual revenue of more than fourteen lacks of rupees.—In this was included the tract of territory which had formerly been allotted to him, in conformity to the will of his father Allee Mahummed, in the firſt general partition made by the guardians. Such of the Afgans, found in arms, as were not immediately attached to Fyzoola Khan, (amounting to about twenty thouſand) together with a very few of their moſt obnoxious leaders, were, by particular ſtipulation, ordered to the weſtward of the Ganges; and marching out of their lines, croſſed that river under the conduct of Ahmed

* Append. No. III. and IV.

Khan Buxy, and other chiefs. These were the only inhabitants of Rohilcund who were expelled from the country in consequence of the war:—the other Rohillas were permitted forthwith to quit their lines and to retire unmolested to their respective places of abode. Although no stipulation was expressed in the treaty for the delivery of any part of the Rohilla property, yet, in consequence of a verbal agreement, and in consideration of the favourable terms which were granted him, Fyzoola Khan paid to the Vizier one half of the treasure in his hands at the period of his surrender, amounting to about fifteen lacks of rupees *.

Fyzoola

* The number of Rohillas banished to the westward of the Ganges by the treaty of Lolldông, amounted (according to the most authentick accounts) to seventeen or eighteen thousand men, (with their families) none being included in the spirit of the treaty, *excepting such as were actually found in arms.* The Hindoo inhabitants, consisting of about *seven hundred thousand*, were no otherwise affected by it than experiencing *a change*

Fyzoola Khan, at his laſt interview with the Vizier, requeſted permiſſion to carry his brother Mahummed-Yâr Khan with him to Rampore, which was immediately granted; the Vizier at the ſame time promiſing, as ſoon as the new arrangements in Kuttâher ſhould be properly adjuſted, to ſettle on him a *Jeyedad* for his future ſupport. This buſineſs being finiſhed, the Rohilla chief retired within a few days after to Rampore (the capital of the diſtricts ſe-

---

change of maſters, to which, in the courſe of the preceding revolutions, they had been frequently accuſtomed.

Having now brought the celebrated *Rohilla war* to a cloſe, it may not be unamuſing to offer to the peruſal of the reader a ſummary of it, as delivered in *another place*.—" The *whole nation*, with inconſiderable ex-
" ceptions, was ſlaughtered or baniſhed.—The coun-
" try was laid waſte with fire and ſword; and that
" land, diſtinguiſhed above moſt others by the *chear-*
" *ful* face of *paternal* government and *protected* labour,
" the choſen ſeat of cultivation and plenty, is now
" throughout a *dreary deſert*, covered with ruſhes and
" briars, and jungles full of wild beaſts ! ! ! *.

* Parliamentary Regiſter, 1781, No. LXXXVI. page 219.

cured to him by the treaty) designing to make it the place of his future residence.—He carried with him five thousand Rohilla soldiers, whom he was allowed by the treaty to retain in his service. The English troops commenced their march down the country at the same time; but, at the request of the Vizier, they halted for some weeks at Ramghaut, in order to be a check upon the neighbouring powers, in case of their making any attempts upon these provinces before they should be restored to permanent tranquillity.

A chief part of the Vizier's troops were dispersed over the different districts of Rohilcund to secure the new conquests; whilst two of his generals, Hîmmet Behâdur and Amrao Gheêr, were detached over the Ganges to Ferrochabâd, where the weak and unhappy representative of the Bungish family, who had already given up his independence, agreed to pay an annual tribute to Suja-al-Dowlah and his successors, and not to keep any force of his own, but to trust

truſt the protection of his territory, and the collection of his revenues to the troops and Aumils of the Nabob of Owde.

Suja-al-Dowlah accompanied the army on their return as far as Biſeghaut, from whence he proceeded to Biſſoolee, and from thence to Fyzabâd, where he died ſhortly after, in conſequence of a diſorder with which he had been long afflicted; and was ſucceeded by his eldeſt ſon Mirza Amânee, under the title of *Aſuph-al-Dowlah*.

This event, which only twelve months before might have excited the moſt violent commotions, was not now attended with the ſmalleſt obſtruction or diſorder. Suja-al-Dowlah, conſcious of his approaching end, had made a diſpoſition of his forces, as well for the ſecurity of his old dominions, as for that of his late acquiſitions; and had taken every neceſſary precaution for the preſervation of the publick tranquillity, with that good judgement and ſound policy which marked his character. But nothing, perhaps, more effectually contributed to these ends than the subjugation of Rohilcund. Had not that expedition taken place, Hafiz Rahmut and the other Afgan chiefs, who were eager to seize on all opportunities for their aggrandizement, would not have failed to blow into a flame that spirit of tumult and sedition which, in eastern governments, constantly attends the succession of an inexperienced young man, in hopes of gaining something amidst the general confusion.——In Suja-al-Dowlah's court existed a number of parties of opposite interests and inclinations; one faction in particular was suspected to be devoted to his second son, whom the Rohilla leaders, either for percuniary reward, or the cession of a small portion of territory, would have readily agreed to assist in the destruction of his elder brother; and the undisturbed facility with which Asuph-al-Dowlah attained his inheritance may be regarded as the first good effect of the subjugation of the Afgan power.

Fyzoola Khan, on his arrival at Rampore, ſettled upon his brother Mahummed Yâr an annuity of fifty thouſand rupees; but the latter did not long enjoy the fruits of his brother's generoſity, as he had been for ſome time paſt afflicted with the ſtone, of which diſorder he died in December, 1774.

Fyzoola Khan, now the only remaining ſon of Allee Mahummed, was certainly a conſiderable gainer by the terms of the peace with Suja-al-Dowlah; as he thereby ſecured to himſelf the actual poſſeſſion of as much territory as he could ever have held under the Rohilla government according to his father's will, and more than double in value and extent, of what he had been ſuffered to enjoy under the adminiſtration of his guardians: nor can he be in the leaſt apprehenſive that his rights, expreſſed in the treaty, ſhould be liable to infringement at any future period, whilſt he continues to conduct himſelf with propriety, as the whole was, in the moſt ſolemn manner, ratified in the name of the East-India Company, by the British commander in chief*. The countries ceded to Fyzoola Khan by the late convention include the districts of Hazrit-Naggûr, Moradabâd, Shawbâd and Rampôre, the most fertile tract in Rohilcund, being an extent of not less than seventy miles in length and thirty in breadth, the annual value of which has been already mentioned. For the protection of this territory he is permitted to keep up such a force as (with the occasional assistance of the English) will afford him an ample defence against invasion; and the tranquil mode of life he has adopted will prevent him from being hastily engaged in any disputes with his neighbours. He with a laudable and unprecedented generosity settled annuities upon

* The reader will be pleased to carry in his mind that this account was wrote above ten years ago.—— Since that period, Fyzoola Khan, doubtful of the validity of the first guarrantee, has procured a new one, under the direct authority of the Bengal government.

the families of ſuch chiefs as had been killed or died in the courſe of the preceding ſervice; and provided in a ſimilar manner for all his principal adherents. He alſo warmly intereſted himſelf in behalf of the families of Hafiz Rahmut and Doondee Khan, (who were confined at Allehabâd *) and at length, aſſiſted by the importunities of Sydoola Khan's Begum, with the Nabob, and the mediation of Mr. Briſtow, the Britiſh reſident in Oude, procured their releaſe, together with that of all the other Rohilla priſoners, on paying a ſmall ranſom.

The family of Hafiz Rahmut, on their releaſe, proceeded to Lucknow, where they took up their reſidence under the protection of the Begum, who had intereſted herſelf in obtaining their freedom; and the houſe of Sefdar Jung (the Vizier's uncle) was, at her inſtance, given up for their accommodation.

---

* See page 252.

Mahboola

Mahboola, and the other defcendants of Doondee Khan, remained fome time at Lucknow, and were afterwards permitted to proceed to Kuttâher, where they now live.*

Zâbita Khan, who is poffeffed of an active and enterprizing genius, although he loft that portion of his country which lay to the eaftward of the Ganges, (which fell to Suja-al-Dowlah with the reft of Rohilcund) yet ftill retains his claim to the poffeffions of his father between that river and the Jumna. He made up a confiderable body of troops out of that part of the Rohilla army which had been ordered acrofs the Ganges agreeably to the convention of Lolldông; and with thefe, fome *Sics*, and other adventurers, he has for fome years paft made himfelf of confiderable confequence in that quarter.—He has at different times endeavoured to make little predatory expe-

* Here the Rohilla narrator finifhes his ftory.

ditions

ditions into Rohilcund at the ſeaſon when the Ganges is fordable in thoſe parts ; but his force is not ſufficiently powerful either in number or quality to render him any way formidable to his ſouthern neighbours *.

Of the other chiefs it is needleſs to ſay any thing particularly.—Totally deprived of that ſelf-created conſequence which they had for a few years aſſumed, they have ſunk back into their original inſignificance. ——Many of them have left the country, to ſeek employment and plunder in other parts ; and the few who remain poſſeſs neither the means nor, perhaps, the incli-

* Since this account was written, Zâbita Khan, in conſequence of the death of Nudjuff Khan, acquired a conſiderable lead in affairs at Delhi, which he would ſtill have retained, had not the Mahrattas again interfered in that quarter.——He died very lately, and has been ſucceeded by his ſon Goolâm Kâdir Khan, under the title of Nijeeb al-Dowlah-Hoſhe-Yâr Jung.

nation,

nation, to awaken the jealoufy of government by exciting difturbances.

The country of Rohilcund, after having, for fome years paft, exhibited nothing but a fcene of repeated devaftation, was at length reftored to permanent tranquillity. The Hindoo farmers, who had been ufed, on every return of the dry feafon, to fee their dwellings deftroyed and their lands laid wafte by bands of foreign depredators, againft whom their factious and turbulent mafters had not the power to defend them, have fince enjoyed their poffeffions in fecurity and repofe; as, except the trifling and momentary incurfions of Zâbita Khan and the *Sics* above remarked, thefe provinces have been preferved in the moft perfect peace during the laft twelve years: a happinefs which it may be with truth affirmed they had not for half a century before experienced.

Evident marks of the turbulence of former times are ftill to be feen:—thefe, however,

ever, appeared in the towns and cities of *Kuttâber*, long before the revolution which gave that country to our ally; nor can this be deemed ſurprizing, if we conſider the ſtate of this territory, continually ſubjected, as it was, either to the diſtraction of inteſtine broils, or the devaſtation of foreign invaſion.—The exertions of Allee Mahummed, the ſtruggles of the Fowjedars, and the efforts of Sefdar Jung in ſupport of the Imperial authority, (which reduced the Rohillas expreſsly to the ſame ſtate in which they ſtood at the period of the Lolldông convention) together with the incurſions of the Mahrattas in later times, all contributed to produce this effect. Some part of this apparent decay, indeed, muſt be attributed to the ſudden and total overthrow of two opulent and powerful families*, the circulation of whoſe wealth gave

* Thoſe of *Hafiz Rahmut* and *Doondee Khan*.—The reader will readily perceive that theſe obſervations are of a date conſiderably later than the preceding part of the

gave life to the cities they inhabited, and whose ostentatious magnificence appeared in the erection of *baths*, mosques and palaces, which are now falling to ruin.—— With respect to the bulk of the inhabitants, it is probable they have been but little effected by the various revolutions their country has experienced.—The cause of this has been already in part explained;* neither should we be too hasty in forming disadvantageous comparative conclusions, from a reflection on the evils which may appear to attend their *present* state,—evils which are to be attributed to a defective administration, capable of correction and amendment, and not to any consequences *necessarily* resulting from the last of these revolutions:—and, in fact, if this territory has been negligently or oppressively governed

the work, which, however, it would be highly improper to bring to a close without a few cursory remarks, not only on the *immediate*, but also, on the present more *remote* effects, of the transactions here recorded.

* In the *Introductory View*.

since

ſince its reduction, (as it moſt certainly has been at times, and in various degrees) it is not probable that it was much better governed, whilſt under the uncertain rule of many contending maſters, with that rule often ſhifting from *one* to *another*:— and if we add to this the circumſtance of the country being, during its firſt adminiſtration, involved in a ſtate of almoſt perpetual hoſtility, we cannot ſuppoſe that a revolution which put a period to theſe calamitous diſturbances can have deducted from the felicity of the inhabitants!—— Strong ideas, indeed, have been conceived (and propagated with the moſt hyperbolical exaggeration) of the ſuperior happineſs of the natives of *Kuttâher* under their *former* Lords, from parallels drawn between the preſent ſtate of the *other* parts of this country, and that of the particular portion of it under the immediate adminiſtration of Fyzoola Khan.——But before we proceed to form a determinate judgement upon grounds which are certainly calculated to miſlead the ſuperficial obſerver, it may be proper

proper to enter into a more diſcriminating inveſtigation of the particular contingencies in which this difference originates.

Not to remark the very ſuperior ſtate of cultivation and population which prevails in the principality of Rampore would be an injuſtice to its proprietor:—it muſt, however, be at the ſame time acknowledged, that as much of this ſuperiority is owing to a happy concurrence of favourable circumſtances, as to any perſonal exertion on the part of its ruler; and is ſuch, in fact, as no exertion whatever could have effected independent of them.

The diſtrict of Rampore, it is true, owes its actual proſperity to the induſtry and ability of Fyzoola Khan;—not, indeed, to theſe qualities, wholly, as the *means*, but to them wholly, in the application of the advantages which he derived from adventitious cauſes.——Firſt, his ſituation;—his territory being defended on one ſide by the Ganges, as well as the interjacent country of Rohilcund (as the above river is about thirty-five miles diſtant from his weſtern frontier)—and the weakneſs of his neighbours lying beyond it ;—on the other ſide and behind, by woods and mountains ;—and on the ſouth, by the protection of the Britiſh, virtually ſaving him from the certain deſtruction which muſt have been his lot, had not the *preſumption* more than the *exertion* of this ſafeguard prevented any attempts to effect it.—— Secondly,—the natural advantages which a *ſmall* dominion enjoys over a *large* (excluſive of the peculiar compactneſs and defenſibility of *his)* in admitting the ſuperintendency of its firſt magiſtrate, without any delegation of official authority, as well in the *general management* as in the *complete controul* of its detail, both of government, revenue, and expence.—— Thirdly,—in a multitude of little ſtreams which fall from the ſurrounding mountains, and fill with every diſſolution of the ſnows above, yielding, with the aid of artificial

tificial dams, a conſtant and unfailing ſupply of moiſture to the neighbouring grounds, in ſeaſons of univerſal drought, as in the years 1781, 2, and 3, when all the upper regions of Hindoſtan were burnt up by the failure of three ſucceſſive rainy ſeaſons; and the cultivation of Rampore was maintained equal to that which it poſſeſſed with the natural influence of the climate.——And—laſtly,—in the ſuperior population, and conſequent cultivation and wealth it derived from the acceſſion of ſubjects, within the three before-mentioned years, from the circumjacent country, (which was not ſo happily circumſtanced in the above eſſential points) as it is natural for men to fly from *famine*, and its inevitable conſequence, *oppreſſion*, to a mild and equal government, and abundance;—and, in the ſame proportion as the territory of Fyzoola Khan *gained* by this circumſtance, that of the Vizier *loſt* in its *population*, and conſequently in its *cultivation* and *revenue*.

Many circumſtances have heretofore concurred

concurred to prevent or interrupt the operation of the interference of the Britiſh government in the correction and amendment of thoſe particular grievances under which the inhabitants of theſe diſtricts labour.—The accumulated diſtreſſes of an univerſal war; the immediate and urgent wants of a government ſtruggling under imminent dangers and almoſt inſuperable difficulties;—and above all, the perpetual ſtruggles of *parties*, either in India or in England, in their effects weakening its influence, circumſcribing its authority, and embarraſſing all its meaſures, have hitherto united to render abortive any efforts which might have been made for this purpoſe.——That means might be adopted, in its preſent ſtate of uninterrupted tranquillity, to reform the abuſes which have heretofore prevented the inhabitants of *Kuttáber* from enjoying the fulleſt advantages of a ſituation happier, in ſome reſpects, than it perhaps ever was in before, cannot be doubted; nor is there any reaſon to deſpair, in the preſent ſtate of the Britiſh goverment in India, of theſe means being ſpeedily and effectually exerted.

Thus have we traced the progreſs of theſe Afgans in the northern provinces, from their firſt riſe under the gallantry and good conduct of Allee Mahummed, through a variety of fortune, to the final diſſolution of their power in Rohilcund by the transfer of the dominion of that diſtrict to Suja-al-Dowlah and his ſucceſſors.

Various and ſevere are the ſtrictures which have been paſſed upon the latter part of thoſe tranſactions, and the prejudice of ignorance and violence of party, aided by the ſtrong aſſertions of popular declamation, have united to make it the ſubject of general odium: but by a reference to the *facts* recited in the foregoing narrative, a more accurate and, i is to be preſumed, a *fairer* judgement may be formed of it.

But, to enter fully into all the reflections which

which occur upon this ſubject would carry the compiler far beyond his original intention, which was only to give an *impartial* and, as far as lay in his power, an *accurate* relation of facts ; and if the peruſal of theſe ſhall tend to eradicate a ſingle prejudice, or remove a ſingle error, with reſpect to the judgement which has hitherto been too generally paſſed upon the latter part of thoſe tranſactions, in which the honour and intereſt of Great Britain are ſo materially and intimately concerned, and the deciſion upon which involves every thing that can be dear to the feelings and the characters of the actors in it, he ſhall think himſelf fully recompenſed for the trouble he has taken.

APPENDIX.

(N°. I.)

TRANSLATION of a Treaty entered into between the Vizier of the Empire Suja-al-Dowlah, and the Rohilla Sirdars, reciprocally interchanged.

AGREEMENT—First, friendship is established " between us; and Hafiz Rahmut and all the other " Rohillas, great and small, have agreed and deter- " mined with the Vizier of the Empire, Suja-al-Dow- " lah, that we adhere to the substance of this writing, " and never deviate from this agreement; that we " esteem his friends as our friends, and his enemies as " our enemies; and that we and our heirs, during our " lives, shall adhere firmly to this our oath and " agreement; that we shall be united and joined to-

" gether for the protection of the country of the Vi-
" zier of the Empire, and of our own country; and
" if any enemy (which God forbid!) should make an
" attempt against us and the Vizier, we the Rohilla
" Sirdars and the Vizier of the Empire shall use
" our joint endeavours to oppose him. We, all the
" Rohilla Sirdars, shall also join and unite in any
" measure that may be determined by the Vizier of
" the Empire for the benefit of the Nabob Mahûm-
" med Zâbita Khan.——We, both parties, swear by
" the Almighty, his Prophet, and the sacred *Koran*,
" that we will firmly adhere to this solemn agree-
" ment, nor ever deviate from this our treaty.

" This Treaty, confirmed by oath, and sealed in
" the presence of General Sir Robert Barker, written
" on the 11th of the month Ribbee-al-Sanee, in the
" 1186th year of the Higera, and in the year of
" Christ 1772."

(N°. II.)

TRANSLATION of a Treaty entered into by Hafiz Rahmut Khan (on the part of the Rohilla Sirdars) with the Nabob Suja-al-Dowlah, Vizier of the Empire.

" THE Vizier of the Empire, Suja-al-Dowlah, " ſhall eſtabliſh the Rohillas in their different poſſeſ- " ſions, obliging the Mahrattas to retire, either by " peace or war;—this to depend on the pleaſure of the " Vizier.

" If at any time, without either peace or war, the " Mahrattas, on account of the rains, ſhall croſs [the " Ganges] and retire, and after the rainy ſeaſon they " ſhould again enter the country of the Rohillas, their " expulſion is the buſineſs of the Vizier.

" The Rohilla Sirdars, in conſequence of the above, " do agree to pay to the Vizier Suja-al-Dowlah *forty* " *lacks of rupees*, in the following manner.

" As the Mahrattas are now in the country of the " Rohilla Sirdars, the Vizier of the Empire ſhall ad- " vance from Shawbad as far as may be neceſſary to " enable

" enable the families of the Rohillas to leave the " jungles and return to their habitations.—Ten lacks " of rupees in ſpecie, in part of the above ſum, ſhall " then be paid; and the remaining thirty lacks in " three years from the beginning of the year 1180 " Fûſſillee.

" This agreement ſealed in the preſence of General " Sir Robert Barker," &c. &c.

N°. III.

(N°. III.)

TRANSLATION of a Treaty under the seal of the Nabob Suja-al-Dowlah, Vizier-al-Mumâleck-Behâdur, and Colonel Alexander Champion, commander in chief of the Company's forces on the expedition against Rohilcund, executed in camp near Lolldông on the 12th of the month Rujib, in the 1188th year of the Higera (the 7th of October, 1774.

" PEACE being concluded between us and the " Nabob Fyzoola Khan Behâdur, I have agreed to " give him the country of Rampore and its depen- " dencies, producing together the yearly sum of " fourteen lacks and seventy-five thousand rupees; " and I have furthermore stipulated that Fyzoola " Khan may retain in his service an armed force con- " sisting of five thousand men, and not a single man " more. I therefore give this written engagement, " that I will, at all times, and upon all occasions, " support the honour and character of the said Fy- " zoola Khan, and will promote his interest and ad-

" vantage

" vantage to the utmoſt of my power,—upon the " following conditions. That Fyzoola Khan ſhall not " enter into connection with any perſon but myſelf; " and that he ſhall hold no correſpondence with any " except myſelf and the Engliſh chiefs; that he ſhall " conſider my friends as his friends, and my enemies " as his enemies: and that, with whomſoever I " ſhall make war, Fyzoola Khan ſhall ſend two or " three thouſand men, according to his ability, to join " my forces; and, if I march in perſon he ſhall him-" ſelf accompany me with his troops, and if, on ac-" count of the ſmallneſs of the number of the forces " he is to retain in his ſervice he be not able to accom-" pany me, I will then appoint him three or four " thouſand more troops, that he may accompany me " with a good army;—and I will be at the expence of " ſupporting them.

" Upon the performance of theſe conditions, I " have agreed to give the ſaid countries, at the afore-" mentioned revenue, to Fyzoola Khan, and to pro-" mote his intereſt and advantage to the utmoſt of my " power.

" If Fyzoola Khan fulfils the articles of this " treaty, and ſteadily adheres thereto, I will not " (God willing) neglect whatever may be to his ad-" vantage. He ſhall ſend the remainder of the Ro-" hillas to the other ſide of the Ganges.

" I have

"I have ſworn upon the holy Koran, calling God "and his Prophet to witneſs to the performance of "theſe articles."

"Executed in the preſence of Colonel Alexander "Champion, as aforeſaid," &c. &c. &c.

No. IV.

(Nº. IV.)

TRANSLATION of a Treaty under the feal of Fyzoola Khan Behâdur and Colonel Alexander Champion, executed at the camp near Lolldông on the 12th of the month Rujib, in the 1188th year of the Higera (the 7th of October, 1774).

" PEACE being concluded between the Vizier-al-" Mumâleck and me, and the Nabob Vizier having " been gracioufly pleafed to beftow on me a country, " I have fworn upon the holy Koran, calling God " and his Prophet to witnefs to what I engage, that " I will always whilft I live continue in fubmiffion " and obedience to the Nabob Vizier; that I will re-" tain in my fervice five thoufand men, ftipulated by " the Nabob Vizier, and not a fingle man more; that " with whomfoever the Nabob Vizier fhall engage in " hoftilities, I will affift him; and, that if the Nabob " Vizier fhall fend an army againft any enemy, I will " perfonally attend him with my forces where he " goes himfelf upon fuch fervice;—or I fhall other-" wife fend two or three thoufand of my troops to " join them;—that I will have no connection with " any perfon but the Nabob Vizier, and will hold no " correfpondence with any one, the Englifh chiefs

" excepted;—

"excepted;—that whatever the Nabob directs I will "execute, and that I will, in all places, and at all "times, whether in prosperity or adversity, continue "his associate.

"I have sworn on the holy Koran, calling God "and his Prophet to witness, to the performance of "these articles.

"May God and his Prophet punish me if I act "contrary to them, or neglect to fulfil the whole of "these conditions."

"Executed in the presence of Colonel Champion as "aforesaid," &c. &c. &c.

(N°. V.)

TRANSLATION of a *Firman* under the seal of Nabob Suja-al-Dowlah, Vizier-al-Mumâleck-Behâdur.

L. | Vizier al Mumâleck
Suja-al-Dowlah
Behâdur. | *S.*

"TO the Chowdries, Collectors, Cânongoes, "Tax-gatherers, Farmers, &c. &c. of the Purgunnas of Shawbâd and Rampore,——Know ye! "that we have granted the jagheers of the under-"mentioned districts to the Nabob Fyzoola Khan "Behâdur, and that the usual and fixed revenues are "to be paid into the hands of the proper officers of "the said Fyzoola Khan;—obeying him in all "things, you shall no way fail in your duty to him "but in every respect submit to his authority.

"Written on the 7th of the month Shaban, in "the 1188th year of the Higera."

Districts, Revenues, and Taxes.

District	Revenue	
Hazrit Naggurr - - -	275,000	Total 14 Lacks and 75,000 Rupees.
Balass Poor - - - - - -	150,000	
Ahaloon - - - - - -	225,000	
Shawbâd - - - - - - -	600,000	
Moradabad - - - - - -	150,000	
At'hud - - - - - - -	75,000	

FINIS.

www.ingramcontent.com/pod-product-compliance
Lightning Source LLC
Chambersburg PA
CBHW021214270326
41929CB00010B/1133

* 9 7 8 3 3 3 7 2 8 7 2 6 9 *